Don't Get Married ... Unless

Know when, to whom, and IF you should tie the knot—and how to fortify your marriage once you do.

Lorraine M. Wright, RN, PhD

www.lorrainewright.com

Don't Get Married...Unless is an expression of the Author's opinions and insights based on her clinical and personal experience and research. Examples herein are compilations and/or fictionalized accounts of real life encounters the Author has experienced. Names have been changed to protect the identities of those involved.

Library and Archives Canada Cataloguing in Publication

Wright, Lorraine M., 1944-
Don't get married-- unless : know when, to whom, and if you should tie the knot-- and how to fortify your marriage once you do / by Lorraine M. Wright.

Includes bibliographical references.
Issued also in an electronic format.
ISBN 978-1-897530-38-2

1. Marriage. 2. Married people--Psychology. 3. Marital quality. I. Title.

HQ734.W9456 2013   306.872   C2013-901695-3

Published by 4th Floor Press, Inc.
www.4thfloorpress.com
1st Printing 2013
Printed in Canada

Don't Get Married ... Unless

Know when, to whom, and IF you should tie the knot—and how to fortify your marriage once you do.

Lorraine M. Wright, RN, PhD

www.lorrainewright.com

Other Books by Lorraine M. Wright:

Wright, L.M., & Leahey, M. (2013). *Nurses and families: A guide to family assessment and intervention* (6th ed.). Philadelphia, PA: F.A. Davis. (Previous editions: 1st ed. 1984; 2nd ed. 1994; 3rd ed. 2000; 4th ed. 2005; 5th ed. 2009). Translations in French, German, Icelandic, Portuguese, Japanese, Spanish and Swedish.

Wright, L.M., & Bell, J.M. (2009). *Beliefs and illness: A model for healing*. Calgary, AB: 4th Floor Press. Translation in Japanese.

Wright, L.M. (2005). *Spirituality, suffering, and illness: Ideas for healing*. Philadelphia, PA: F.A. Davis. Translations in Portuguese and Japanese.

Wright, L.M., Watson, W.L., & Bell, J.M. (1996). *Beliefs: The heart of healing in families and illness*. New York, NY: Basic Books. Translations in Japanese and Swedish.

Bell, J.M., Watson, L.W., & Wright, L.M. (Eds.). (1990). *The cutting edge of family nursing*. Calgary, AB: Family Nursing Unit Publications.

Bell, J.M., Wright, L.M., Leahey, M., Watson, W.L., & Chenger, P.L. (Eds.). (1988). *International family nursing conference proceedings*. University of Calgary, Calgary, AB.

Leahey, M., & Wright, L.M. (Eds.). (1987). *Families and life-threatening illness*. Springhouse, PA: Springhouse.

Leahey, M., & Wright, L.M. (Eds.). (1987). *Families and psychosocial problems*. Springhouse, PA: Springhouse.

Wright, L.M., & Leahey, M. (Eds.). (1987). *Families and chronic illness*. Springhouse, PA: Springhouse.

Dedication

To my dear niece, Marcy J. Wright, for finding the courage to love again.

Acknowledgements

Although I have published nine academic books, this was my first attempt at writing a self-help book. I would not have been able to enter into this new venue of writing without the expert guidance and competence of Anne Bougie-Johnson, Vice-President and Literary Agent for 4th Floor Press, Inc., Calgary, Canada. Her patience, encouragement, wisdom, humour, and amazing developmental editing has enabled me to finally complete this ten-year project. She has been a joy to work with once again. My heartfelt thanks for being there, Anne, throughout this long process.

To Johanna Bates, President and Founder of 4th Floor Press, Inc., Calgary, Canada, I also wish to give my sincere thanks. You believed in this book from our very first meeting ten years ago and patiently, oh so patiently, waited for the manuscript.

To Wendy Lukasiewicz, Copy Editor, 4th Floor Press, Inc., who once again capably and efficiently readied this manuscript for production.

To my wonderful single, married, widowed, and divorced friends and family members, I acknowledge and am so grateful for your love and support in my various professional endeavours. Some of you have been in and out of love, some of you have been in and out of marriage, some of you desire marriage and some not, some of you love marriage and some not, but all of you have taught me ever so much about love and marriage.

Specifically, I have learned much from and wish to thank:

Family members:

My dear mother, Hazel (deceased), and father, Jim (58 years of marriage); my father and Marge (10 years of marriage); my maternal grandmother (Nanny), Elizabeth J. Doran Schollar (deceased); my grandparents, Bob and Gertrude Wright (both deceased); my brother and sister-in-law, Bob and Carol Wright; niece Marcy and husband, Kenny; nephew Doran and wife, Erin; nephew Ryan and wife, Liz; Uncle Jim (deceased) and

Auntie Dorothy; and Uncle Ray (deceased) and Roy (deceased) (partners for 47 years); and Uncle Ray (deceased) and Claude (partners for 6 years) and cousins Sharon, Pat and husband Peter.

Canadian and International Friends (Single, Married, Divorced, Widowed, and some who have passed but left me with great learnings about love, marriage, and relationships):

Anne Marie and Ingo; Alisha and David; Barbara and Terry (both deceased); Fabie and Jean-Marie; Giezelle and Michael; Janet and Barry; Janice and Curtis; Kat and Calvin; Luísa and Joaquim; Maria do Ćeu and Delfim; Marsha and Michael (deceased); Maureen and Douglas; Michiko and Yoshiharu; Myrna and Bill (deceased); Verone and Eric; and Beverly, Birte, Britt-Inger, Chintana, Dimitrana, Elaine, Erla, Eva, Jerry, Joanne, Margaretha, Martin, Merv, Nami, Nancy, Patrick, Rachel (deceased), Sheldon, Suntharavadee, Suzanne, Thelma (deceased), Vivian (deceased), Wannee, and Wendy.

Colleagues:

Many colleagues have influenced me by their dedication and devotion to understanding, researching, counselling, and/or writing about love, marriage, and/or marital therapy. I admire each of you for your knowledge, wisdom, and desire to save marriages.

Specifically, I wish to thank Dr. Janice Bell, Dr. Evan Imber Black, Dr. Fabie Duhamel, Maggie Gallagher, Dr. John Gottman, Dr. Maureen Leahey, Giezelle Pash, Dr. Wendy L. Watson Nelson, Dr. Frank Pittman (deceased), Terry Real, Dr. John Rolland, Diane Sollee, Dr. Steven Stosny, Dr. Karl Tomm, Linda J. Waite, Sheldon Walker, Dr. Froma Walsh, and Michelle Weiner-Davis. I am also very grateful to the late Gordon B. Hinckley, President of the Church of Jesus Christ of Latter-Day Saints, for his wisdom and counsel about marriage.

Graduate students:

My students at the University of Calgary have always shown such enthusiasm and generosity for my ideas of assisting couples who were suffering in their marriage. My "5 Hot Tips" for marriage became a favourite for their own lives, and those hot tips are now woven into this book. I thank those students who continually encouraged me to write this book.

Finally, to the **good men** that I have dated in my life: I am grateful for your kindness, thoughtfulness, intellect, humour, and wonderful memories. There has not been a rogue among you.

Lorraine M. Wright, Calgary, Alberta, Canada

TABLE OF CONTENTS

Author's Note

Marriage isn't supposed to make you happy—it's supposed to make you married.

—Frank Pittman

Since I have not yet married, and perhaps never will, I wish to acknowledge and thank all those family members, friends, clients, colleagues, and graduate students who have taught me about marriage and especially those who encouraged me to write this book.

The greatest learning about marital dynamics, with all its simplicity and complexity, has come from the many couples I have had the privilege of counselling over some forty years. I am grateful for their openness and stories of anguish and triumph, pain and ecstasy, hope and despair. In my early years as a marital and family therapist, I was often asked, "Are you married?" This was legitimate; I was a novice at assisting those who were suffering in their marriages. As the years passed, I was rarely asked that question and nowadays, never. Competence in dealing with marriages that are off the rails has trumped not having my own personal experience in marriage.

I am particularly grateful to those sincere souls who sought to earnestly renew and revive their marriages. We worked hard to achieve their goal of saving their marriages, and, in the majority of cases, we did just that.

All of you taught me that marriage can bring the greatest joy and the greatest angst of all human relationships. The couples described in this book are either actual couples I had the privilege of working with (their names and sometimes location and/or ethnicity changed for confidentiality) or are composites of couples with whom I have worked.

I began writing this book while visiting my father and his bride, who had then only been married three months. As a daughter, I was grateful that my eighty-year-old father had married someone older than me! I was even more grateful that his three years of loneliness following the death of my dear mother would now be softened. It seemed quite fitting to be in their presence for a couple of weeks while beginning to immerse myself in writing about when **NOT** to marry. At the time of finishing this book, the newlyweds have enjoyed ten years of marriage.

My father's courtship with his new wife lasted only six weeks before they were engaged. The engagement was a mere four months. When he phoned to tell me the big news, I couldn't resist some teasing: "I hope if I become engaged in just six weeks you'll be as supportive of me as I am of you."

My father, always quick with a witty response, said, "At our age you can't wait too long; we could be dead next year." Yes, at their age, a long courtship and engagement may not have been practical, but they were also veterans of marriage with a great track record. Both had honoured their marriage vows of "in sickness and in health" and had been caregivers to their first spouses. Neither had been divorced or separated.

Both believed their first marriages had been happy and successful. My parents had been married for fifty-eight years, and his new wife had been married for forty-six. They had learned what it takes to have a fortified marriage. I believe that the success of their first marriages made it easier for them to more readily give their love away to another once again.

I couldn't help but wonder if they were marrying for companionship, love, or both. I must admit that I was quite naïve about later-life marriages, and I assumed they had married only for companionship. But not this couple. They informed me that they married for companionship *and* for love. They both agreed that they could not have married only for companionship. As my father tells it, "Well, the bottom line is, we fell in love!"

Yes, love must be the context and framework for any successful and meaningful relationship. But is love enough? Can you marry someone who isn't "right for you," even if you love him or her? How does a couple know that they are right for each other?

In the conversation that followed, the newlywed couple offered some wise counsel about courtship and marriage. I suppose that 104 years of experience gives you something to say. It was particularly fascinating that their beliefs about what makes a satisfying marriage were congruent with my observations as a marital therapist.

I asked them, "When should you never marry, even if you're in love?"

Without hesitation or equivocation, they said, "Never marry anyone who is physically, emotionally, or mentally abusive."

"And don't mess with anyone who has an alcohol, drug, or gambling problem," my father continued.

After marriage, they believed those types of problems would only become worse. They also stated that you need to know each other's spending habits and cautioned against marrying anyone who is deeply in debt.

"How long should you date or be engaged to learn about a potential partner?" I asked.

"One year," they said firmly. Living together prior to marriage was not part of their value system when they were young or then in their twilight years.

"What's the difference between marriage in later life and marriage when you are young?"

They agreed that a later-life marriage was much "easier." What made it easier? "No stress, no job pressure, no kids to raise, no trying to succeed in your profession and not paying enough attention to your marriage. You just get up every day and make a plan to have fun together."

"What makes a marriage successful at any age?"

"Good communication. Talk to one another. You cannot assume. There has to be give and take. Jack Spratt would eat no fat, his wife would eat no lean." Yes, there may be differences, but they believe they can be manageable, negotiable, and tolerable. They didn't think marriage should be age-driven anyway; rather, it should be situational. "Each should be on their own for a while," they said, meaning living away from their parents and providing for themselves. My father advised that you need to "love another for who they are, not for who you would like them to be . . ." His new wife embellished this idea: "Eventually you grow and change together, but you cannot demand change. It must come spontaneously."

Of course, I couldn't resist asking them a

question that plagues our society, and even plagues me as a marriage and family therapist. "What do you believe is the main cause of divorce?" Their answer was simple: "Lack of commitment and responsibility." This newlywed couple believes that everything flows from these two qualities. There would be "no affairs, financial mismanagement, or many other problems if couples were truly committed and responsible to one another."

This conversation was a springboard for writing about my own professional experiences. In a sober, excited, and reverent manner, I am sharing the knowledge I've gleaned about this wonderful thing called **marriage**.

Introduction

They do not love who do not show their love.

—William Shakespeare

I believe many, maybe even most, men and women should *not* marry. This may seem radical, perhaps even anti-marriage, but I don't think of myself as a radical person. I'm quite conservative and I'm certainly not against marriage. However, after forty years of counselling couples, I am convinced that the majority of men and women, particularly in North America, simply do not have the "right stuff" or the "right spirit" for marriage. They don't have the ability to consider another before themselves, which is why they cannot commit to or be successful in marriage. Most individuals believe they are ready for marriage simply because they have reached a typical marrying age or have found someone they would like to marry or are "in love" with. But my professional and personal life experiences have shown me that most people considering marriage are just too underdeveloped, too selfish, too self-absorbed, too self-centred, or just too immature for the gargantuan task of sharing their lives with an equal partner.

All these characteristics are indicators of the most important omission—the inability to give their love away. That's right, *to give their love away*. Most of us are waiting for love, longing for love, wishing for love, and praying for love to come to us. We aren't looking for opportunities to give our love away. We're seeking to get love. When we do look to give love, we put conditions on it. We only want to give our love away *after* we have been shown love or told we are loved. We've got it all backwards.

Love isn't a "thing" out there waiting to find us; it's a biological and spiritual phenomena that we give away. Giving our love away for the sheer joy of caring for and loving someone else, **IS** the gift of love. It's not the return of love that makes us blissful. It's giving love away and expecting nothing in return.

You can argue or debate that some marriages get into difficulty because the individuals married too young, had difficult childhoods, or didn't have good role models. Yes, all of these things can be hindrances or obstacles to satisfying marriages, but they are not the main reason why couples inflict pain on one another, treat each other badly, lie, cheat, or deceive. People behave this way because they're too immature. They marry thinking they'll receive unconditional love, without ever having to give it. Then they're surprised when they end up in divorce court. Once married, selfishness, on the part of one or both spouses, is the second major cause of divorce. Selfish people don't appreciate that what goes around comes around.

What is the biggest reason for divorce? What happens to that fifty percent who start out with such high hopes, such ecstacy, only to end up hurt, angry, and demoralized? I believe the number one reason for divorce is choosing the wrong person. And YOU may be the wrong person.

Marriage should be reserved only for those special and incredible individuals who really have the "right stuff" and are prepared to do those things that will guarantee that their marriage is successful, sacred, and completely secure.

It's a mistake to think that everyone deserves

or has the right to be married. If more people who simply aren't good candidates for marriage would not marry, so much heartache and misery (and money!) would be spared. And just think of the self-doubt that would be avoided. You wouldn't ask, "What's wrong with me that he would have an affair?" or "How can she expect me to spend every Christmas with her parents?" or "Why does he criticize me and put me down in front of our friends?" Those who have affairs, are demanding and uncompromising about rituals, or who criticize rather than commend their spouses in front of others, are all examples of individuals who should not be married. They are selfish and immature. Think of the sleepless nights that would be omitted, the grieving of lost hopes and dreams that would be eliminated, and the betrayals that would disappear if more people didn't marry.

Most important of all, think of the children. The thousands and thousands of dear children who would be spared from inconsiderate, insensitive, selfish, and thoughtless parents. These are parents whose needs as individuals are more important than their children's needs. Children wouldn't have to experience the unraveling of a marriage and family. In therapy, I have witnessed over and over again that it is the children who suffer most when they are subjected to immature and selfish parents.

Divorce doesn't happen when one marries the "right person," is the "right person," and then invests in that marriage with commitment and responsibility. This maturity and commitment, combined with a love of a biological, spiritual, and emotional nature, are the winning combination for a successful marriage.

What will happen to all those people who never marry? Sadly, many will go from one relationship to another, seeking someone whom they can control, manipulate, deceive, betray, or abuse. Others will be plagued by unkindness, selfishness, and self-absorption. Not one of these behaviours has any place in a loving marriage. On the other hand, if they're lucky, these singles will recognize this time of their lives as an opportunity for maturing and obtaining the skills that will bring their best selves forward, and to be ready for marriage when love resides in their heart. Will you be one of these? Or will you make the mistake of not knowing yourself well enough to say no to marriage?

If you're not 100 percent sure, I plead with you—do not marry. Do not even think about it . . . UNLESS you're willing to do the work to improve yourself first. If you can't commit to self-improvement, step away from the altar. Please let marriage be for those rare few who have been blessed with the right stuff or who have done the work to learn what that takes. It's difficult to admit you're not ready or not brave enough to face the challenges of becoming so. Unfortunately, few individuals in our North American culture are capable of believing and doing the things that I write about in Part I and Part II.

Part I outlines those blazing red flags that anyone contemplating marriage should be on guard for when choosing a mate. If you have any of these bad behaviours, risky situations, goofy beliefs, or deficit experiences, then of course you are not a candidate for marriage either. You and your partner have a long way to go before taking that step.

Part II explains how marrying the wrong person in the first place is the biggest reason for divorce. How do you know he or she is the wrong person? Check your potential mate against my list and see how they measure up. Do they refuse to introduce you to their family? Is one or both of your families strongly opposed to your relationship? Is either of you unwilling to take a Marriage Education or Marriage Preparation class? Does your mate meet these standards? Do YOU? Are you the wrong person in this relationship?

Once married, you need to be willing and prepared to do certain things to show and demonstrate your love. In Part III, specific ideas, skills, rituals, and advice are offered for what I call a "fortified marriage." Take these steps to ensure your union.

Any successful marriage must ritualize three things: regular time together, regular praise and affection, and regular intimacy. There's nothing magic about these suggestions, but an ongoing miracle happens when they are regularly practiced. Love expands and endures. Marriages remain intact. By following the very specific behaviours and skills I suggest, you will sustain a secure marriage. Finally, I discuss ideas about love that keep it all together, like being able to give your love away and knowing that love will be returned because you have chosen well, prepared well, and learned the skills that help love endure.

It is my hope that this book will challenge current views, ideas, and beliefs about eligible marriage partners, marriage essentials, marital bliss, and marital satisfaction. In my view, there are too many books on the market about how to find a mate, how to have a grand wedding, and how to make a marriage work. But there are far too few books on *NOT* marrying. Marriage is the biggest decision you will ever make in your life. It is not for everyone. Single people may come to appreciate their singleness as a marvellous gift of time in which to grow and improve in order to bring their best selves forward to a marriage relationship, or they may realize that they should not now or *ever* marry.

For those of you already married, I hope this book will give you a renewed appreciation of the advantages, blessings, benefits, and sacredness of marriage. I hope you will be open to reviewing the checklist of what it takes to maintain a successful, satisfying, and sacred marriage.

Part I

Don't Get Married . . . Unless You Can Get Rid of These!

All marriages are incompatible. All marriages are between people from different families, people who have a different view of things. The magic is to develop binocular vision, to see life through your partner's eyes as well as through your own.

—Frank Pittman

Introduction

Bad marriages don't just happen to bad people. They mostly happen to good people who aren't good for each other and didn't have the maturity and skills necessary to embark on a marriage. People must address their bad behaviours, bad habits, and risky situations before they can become a good candidate for marriage and before entering into marriage. For some, goofy beliefs need to be challenged before committing to marriage, while others simply haven't had enough real-life experience to prepare them for marriage. In this section of the book, I will address the most important red flags that can assist you in recognizing if you and/or your current partner are good candidates for marriage or if you have more work to do first.

It takes great maturity and commitment to dissolve the mythology of marriage and instead realize that two individuals need to bring their best selves forward and be the best candidates for a successful marriage. If you recognize these red flags in your relationship, you can acknowledge your issues and work to address them. You will not only increase your chances of a marvellous marriage but will have already eliminated some of the things that can doom your marriage from the start.

Chapter 1

Very Bad Behaviours and Very Bad Manners

Manners are a sensitive awareness of the feelings of others. If you have that awareness, you have good manners, no matter what fork you use.

—Emily Post

Don't Get Married
. . . *If either of you are possessive, jealous, or needy.*

In true trust there is freedom. If you have your partner on a two-inch leash, you're not ready to walk down the aisle. If you feel anxious, fearful, or borderline homicidal when your partner is in the presence of the opposite sex, you're not ready. If you can't let your man go to a football game with his friends, or let your woman have a girls' weekend, you're not ready. It might seem innocent enough to check an email here or there, but it can spiral, fast. Before you know it, you're monitoring all of your partner's emails or text messages, calling their cell phone fifty times a day, then outright stalking. Where does it end?

Loving another is about showing trust. Trust means that you allow, even encourage, your partner to have his or her own experiences, while you enjoy your own experiences and wait to hear about your partner's. Jealousy, possessiveness, or neediness that denies another their freedom to call or to visit friends and family, that forces them to have their lives monitored and watched, or feel as if they're walking on eggshells, is not a relationship built on love and trust, but rather built on insecurity, immaturity, and fear. If you have a penchant for controlling others through your actions of jealousy and/or possessiveness (all the while professing that you're simply watching out for them), please seek counselling and uncover these fears and insecurities. Take a leap in your own life and challenge your beliefs about what it means to trust another.

If you are dating someone with these tendencies, exit left. You can't fix them. These traits are a part of who they are, deep down in their bone marrow. Only working with a competent therapist can help to unravel these insecurities and replace them with more loving and trusting thoughts, emotions, and behaviours.

Fatima came from a large, loud, and loving Portuguese family. She had been married for eleven years to Fayez, an only child. They had two girls, ages nine and six. They came to see me in my clinical practice because of communication problems.

"I don't know why she says we have problems," Fayez said immediately. "I don't have any complaints. Fatima's the one who's always unhappy."

"Don't have problems?" Fatima asked. "You can't stand that I talk to other people . . . anyone, my family, my friends. You act as though I've been unfaithful every time I go to a family dinner, Fayez." She threw her hands up as her voice rose. She turned in her chair to look directly at her husband.

Fayez's feet shuffled against the carpet and the corners of his mouth turned down. It was obvious we weren't going to make any great progress on this first visit.

At our next meeting, Fatima told me that Fayez wouldn't come back to these meetings if she was going to lie about him. He had called her selfish and sick.

"Every time we go to dinner with my family, he complains," Fatima said.

"How often are these dinners?" I asked.

"All the time," Fayez huffed.

"A lot," Fatima grudgingly agreed. "I have a big family and we're very close. We like to see as much of each other as we can. But the minute we get home, he's complaining that I was too loud, that I didn't pay enough attention to him, or that my family doesn't like him. He just goes on and on "

Fayez was an only child and both his parents died prematurely in a car accident. His parents had adored him and expected others to feel the same. As the years passed, he became more and more emotionally violent, calling his wife demeaning names, like "idiot" and "stupid." He tried with all his might to avoid her family and keep Fatima all to himself. He'd make excuses as to why they couldn't socialize with her family, and he often feigned illness if she wanted to go out with their friends.

I chose to see Fayez for some individual sessions. He told me he wanted to save his marriage but had no clue how to do it. We discussed his own family relationships and the anguish of losing his parents at such a young age and then being raised by his aunt and uncle. "My parents doted on me, always made me feel so special. I was everything to them. But then with my aunt and uncle, I was suddenly being raised with four cousins. I was just one of many kids in the house. I didn't feel like I belonged there, that I fit in."

"And that's what you want from your wife?" I asked. "To be the number one person in her life?"

"Yes, that's what I want." He opened his hands, palms up, and looked at them. "But she has so many people in her life, so much family. I'm just one of many, again."

We began to unpack his insecurities, jealousy, and desperate need for a close, loving attachment with his wife. He became less defensive, but he still lacked the necessary skills to behave differently with his wife. I asked him to read the book Love Without Hurt (2005) by Dr. Steven Stosny. He found the ideas in the book incredibly helpful, especially about bringing forth compassion in his relationship. He told me that this was a totally new idea for him, but he still wanted to know WHAT he should do. I find that men like knowing specific tips, tools, and strategies that they can implement to improve their relationships. I told him it was premature to try anything differently until he learned some skills, but perhaps he could just make small efforts to be kind.

"That's all? Sure, I can do that." He smiled.

Over the next months, Fayez began initiating small acts of kindness with his wife. He didn't question Fatima's every movement, and he took the girls to the park so she could work on her online course without disruptions. Most surprisingly, he initiated a barbecue with two other couples. These were huge steps for him, and his wife was in shock. She didn't have the skills to respond to kindness from her own husband.

"Are you okay?" she'd demand. "I've never seen you act like this before. Are you having an affair?"

Of course these kinds of comments from Fatima had to stop immediately. Over the next few months, this couple's progress wasn't exactly a straight line, but rather like the stock market with sharp ups and downs. I wanted Fayez to be open to my ideas, so I moved slowly, asking him to make small changes that would net big results. He needed to realize that he had "bone marrow" issues over the loss and grief of his parents that resulted in his controlling behaviours to secure his wife's love.

The good news is that they have made significant progress. Fayez's Achilles' heel in his marriage is his own attachment issues, which he'll always have to be vigilant about. Fatima needs to continue offering commendations for her husband's behaviour and not drift into also being negative and doubting. Trust in a healthy relationship must flow both ways.

. . . *If either of you have a drug, alcohol, pornography, or gambling problem.*

When given a choice, an addict will always pick their drug of choice over the needs of another human being. When addiction takes hold, it is impossible for the addict to give their full attention or commitment to a spouse. His or her marriage to the bottle, the drug, or the dice will always take priority. You will never be able to compete, so don't even try. Run as fast as you can in the opposite direction.

Sobriety doesn't happen overnight. It's a long and arduous process that requires the addict's constant attention. If a person has been addiction-free for at least twelve months, you *might* consider becoming involved, but nothing less than one year. If you are the person with the addiction, please do not marry! If you are willing to have an intense relationship with a human rather than a thing, then seek treatment immediately. But don't make your spouse play second fiddle in your life. Do not marry until you have mastered your addiction(s).

Alicia and Jason sat in my office. Alicia scowled and her foot tapped the floor in annoyance.

"I begged Alicia to come here," Jason said. "We need help."

Alicia had always been a heavy social drinker. Jason had ignored the signs, and now it was getting out of control. He was desperate for a solution, while his wife saw no reason for intervention. Over the two years they were married, he claimed Alicia's drinking had increased, but his concern escalated with the birth of their daughter, now fourteen months old.

"So what? I like to drink sometimes. He's totally overreacting," Alicia said with a pout that would have better suited a toddler. As their story unfolded, it became obvious to me that Alicia was married more to the bottle than to Jason.

Alicia had been previously married, with no children, and she denied that drinking had been a problem in that marriage. Jason now believed it was the cause for her previous divorce.

"I had heard rumours," Jason interjected, "when we first started dating. But they were just rumours. She didn't drink around me at that point, so I ignored what people were saying."

Alicia looked steadily at the toes of her polished black shoes.

"I should have," he continued. "I should have seen it then, but it was a whirlwind. I fell for Alicia hard and fast. I'd just been dumped, right before her and I met. I guess I was a bit needy. I wanted a relationship and Alicia seemed great."

The pair had cleared a major hurdle when they became engaged. Jason was a member of a religious community (one that abstained from drinking alcohol), but Alicia was not. She converted to Jason's faith prior to their wedding. She affirmed that she would live their married life according to the tenets of her new religious community. Jason figured this covered all the bases, that their marriage would be clean and sober all the years of their lives.

Then it started, slowly.

"We were out for a special dinner, this was while we were engaged. She told me she wanted to have a drink with the meal. She said that, of course, once we were married, she wouldn't drink anymore. She promised she would honour our faith." He swallowed hard, clearing the lump that had formed in his throat, while his wife fidgeted in her chair and rolled her eyes.

"It was just a drink with dinner," she shot at him.

"But it was never just one, was it?" Jason turned to her. "Once you start drinking it doesn't end until you're flat out drunk. I kept telling myself that it would stop after the wedding. But it didn't. Before we married, you were always going out with your single girlfriends till all hours. They'd have to call me in the middle of the night to come get you. Too drunk to make it home on your own. You were always sorry." He turned back to me. "She was always sorry that it had happened. Always promised me the next day that it wouldn't happen again. There was always an excuse. It was her last chance to party with the girls or someone's birthday or some other celebration. But no celebration ever ended with her being sober."

I could tell Alicia was listening but that she wasn't hearing her husband at all. To her, it was just him whining and being oversensitive. For Jason, it was his last ditch attempt at saving their marriage.

"She tried, after the wedding. She really tried not to drink, but it only lasted a couple of months. It started again slowly, with a drink when we were out for dinner—only it wasn't to celebrate anymore. It was because she was stressed from mothering our newborn daughter or because I had done something to upset her. And the nights out with the girls started ending later and later." He shook his head. "I should have seen it then. Should have made her get help."

"But you didn't," I said. "So why now? What's brought you to my office today?"

"I came home from work early one day last week. She was drinking vodka." My eyebrows went up. I know vodka is often the drink of choice for those who are trying to hide that they've been drinking. "She was drinking alone in the afternoon while taking care of our daughter."

"Goodness, it's not like I was drunk," Alicia said.

I wish I could report that this young mother recognized her serious problem, sought treatment, and mastered her addiction. She did none of these things. This marriage ended in despair with Jason deciding to separate and requesting custody of his child. So much suffering could have been avoided if Jason would have acknowledged the red flags prior to their marriage. He saw the drinking, saw the habits she exhibited right up to their wedding day, but ignored them. He thought marriage would be enough to change her.

Unfortunately, Alicia had her own strong intimacy with booze that denied her the chance to experience human intimacy. I hope one day Alicia will recognize that her addiction is holding her back from healthy relationships with others and herself.

. . . If either of you refuse to bathe, brush your teeth, or get regular medical checkups.

Marriage cannot be a bed of roses with a partner who stinks! Yes, I have seen couples in my clinical practice where one or both spouses were not big on personal hygiene. In our North American culture, making love to someone who refuses to bathe is not appealing. In the time of Shakespeare, people were known to bathe only once a year, and in the 1950s only once a week. Luckily, times have changed.

If someone cares so little for their own personal hygiene, you have to wonder how they will care for you if you are sick or need help to bathe yourself. When children enter the picture, who's going to help them brush their teeth or wash their faces? Nope, if your partner hasn't learned to have good hygiene on their own, you don't want to be the soap police.

Leroy and Rayleen were both extreme athletes who had met while hiking in Patagonia, Argentina. During their month-long adventure, they never bathed, let alone encountered a shower. In the context of the rustic setting, this was completely acceptable. They fell in the grip of love and believed they had truly found "the one." They were married just three weeks after returning home. Their plan was to make some fast money and leave on another adventure in six months.

I met this couple three months after they married. Rayleen was shocked that Leroy did not bathe regularly upon returning home, which she believed should be a daily event.

"Oh, come on," Leroy said. "That's totally unnecessary! Showering every day. Ridiculous, honestly. I didn't hear you complaining about me not showering in Patagonia. Hell, you didn't shower while we were there either!"

"Because we were backpacking through the wilderness! I assumed that once we got back to civilization you'd be just as happy to see a shower as I was," she said. "How difficult is it to shower every day? It's not that much of a hardship, but you won't even try. Not even every other day."

"Why should I? It's not like I have anyone to impress. You won't come near me."

"How can you expect me to have sex with you when you stink? It's disgusting!" Her face flushed in anger and embarrassment.

"It's not disgusting, it's natural. Rugged."

In the battle of wills, it was clear neither of them were willing to lose.

A lack of personal hygiene was one of the things Rayleen learned about Leroy when they returned to real life—working every day and dating—but there were also layers of other unmet expectations. Leroy expected that in order to leave North America and travel again as a married couple, all the money they made would be put towards that goal. That meant not spending money on treats or presents for Rayleen's nieces and nephews. No splurges or extras of any kind. To Leroy, this type of frugality defined a good wife. Rayleen did not agree. She ignored these red flags and plunged into the marriage anyway. They separated after just six months.

What is the real issue here, soap or a short courtship away from your home turf? The real issue wasn't hygiene but hopping into a marriage too quickly. Falling in love on adventure trips, cruises, or European holidays all have the same thing in common. It's not real life and so expectations are different. We need to see our potential marriage mate in our own home context and theirs. We need to have a realistic picture of who they are, how they behave around family and friends, and how they handle the day-to-day pressures of life.

Personal hygiene—taking care of one's self—is a reflection of a person's self-worth, self-image, and their priorities in life. It might seem like a quick rinse, but it can be so much more.

. . . If either of you refuse to meet and/or visit your future in-laws.

You're not just marrying him, you're marrying his whole family. If you find this difficult to accept, you're not ready for marriage. Also, if you're being kept a secret from your partner's family, you MUST question why. Do you embarrass him or her, and why would that be? Would family members not approve of your religion, ethnic background, lifestyle, or profession? Or do you have children and feel his or her family would not readily embrace them? If you were loved, your partner would be proud and excited to introduce you to family. If not, he or she believes you will not be accepted. Couples often like to believe that it can be "us against the world," but that never works out if it's "us" against "family."

In Asian, Muslim, and Hispanic families, it would be incredibly rare that future spouses wouldn't be introduced early on in the courtship to their future in-laws. Shelina Zahra Janmohamed's delightful book *Love in a Headscarf* (2009) offers great insight into the dating process in modern

Muslim families, where parents and family often participate in the selection process for finding a spouse. It can be quite a different story for Caucasian people. I have been amazed how some Caucasians actually entertain the idea of NOT having their family meet their future spouse. In fact, some only meet for the first time at the wedding ceremony or not at all. I'll make allowances for those families who are deceased or live in Antarctica and can only get off the ice twice a year. All other circumstances are unacceptable. Marrying without meeting and spending time with your future in-laws is one of the biggest mistakes you can make prior to marriage. Why? Because meeting your partner's family, even if it's just once, will lift the veil from your eyes and make you see and understand your partner in a whole new light. How does he treat his parents, especially the parent of the opposite sex? This one trait can tell you exactly how you will be treated in your marriage—or how your partner will handle a relationship with your children.

No one is an island. Like it or not, you are now part of each other's families.

Martina and Jose wed without Martina ever meeting Jose's parents. He convinced Martina that his parents were too elderly and frail to make the trip from Guatemala to Canada for their wedding. Martina asked many times to at least talk to his parents on the phone or email them prior to their wedding, but these suggestions were met with resistance and excuses. Finally, after five years of marriage, Martina realized that no contact had been made between Jose and his family. She questioned him further.

"Okay, okay, we haven't talked in years," Jose finally admitted, after much badgering. "I wanted to come to Canada. They told me it was a bad idea, that I would fail in a new country, that I shouldn't leave Guatemala."

"That's it?" Martina asked, stunned. "You haven't talked to your own parents for . . . how long? Because they didn't want you to move away from them?"

"Seven years," he answered quietly. "It's been seven years."

"How could you do that to them?"

"They didn't support me," he tried to answer.

"Of all the things I imagined, of all the scenarios I created in my mind about why you refused to introduce me to your family, I never thought it would be something as immature and self-centred as this!"

"Immature? Self-centred?" he said. "They refused to support my decision . . ."

"They cared about you and gave you their opinion. You skulked out of the house and out of the country like a child!"

Martina finally convinced Jose to re-establish contact with his parents. She was now pregnant and wanted them to be able to anticipate this joyous event. Finally, Jose made the call, only to learn that his father had passed away one year earlier. The family hadn't known how to reach Jose. This was not the legacy Martina wanted for her own children—to be cut off from their parents.

The whole family needed to heal. Jose's lies had hurt Martina. She needed to feel that family was as important to him as he had said it was. She didn't trust her husband—not only for the lies but also for the poor choices he had made.

Jose had a lot of work to do. He needed to mend the fences he'd left broken in Guatemala and rebuild the trust between him and his wife. He needed to mature in his ideas of parenting, before the arrival of his own child. He also needed to overcome the guilt of not having been there for his father before he died and to make things right with his mother.

Luckily, Jose's mother was forgiving and happy to finally have contact with her son again. She invited him and Martina to come to Guatemala when the baby was born.

Through Martina's love and encouragement, Jose was now contacting his mother frequently by phone and email, as was Martina. The last time I heard from them they had just returned from a joyous reunion in Guatemala with the new grandchild. What a wasted few years because of Jose's immaturity and lack of skills to learn how to have a relationship with his parents, even if he did not agree with their advice about moving to Canada. He was fortunate to have met and married a wife who "pushed" this issue, resulting in reconciliation. But oh, the hurt and years of anguish that could have been avoided.

Don't marry someone who is not proud to introduce you and welcome you into their family. You'll never be able to guess their true reasons—and those reasons could end up having a major impact on your life.

. . . If either of you have children but do not accept emotional, financial, or geographical responsibility for them.

Children add a whole other level of complexity to any relationship. If you are contemplating marrying someone with children, you need to think long and hard. Yes, sometimes it works and works well. But to be successful, it requires incredible maturity, flexibility, and security on the part of the non-biological "parent" or step-parent. Most biological parents will always side with their children over a new step-parent. And that's the way it should be. As a partner to someone with children, you should be a consultant, never a replacement, to the biological parent. If both of you have children from previous unions, this simply adds to the level of complexity and the number of relationships. Of course, there are stories where the joining of partners with their children is bliss, but more often it is a battleground of unclear boundaries, unmet expectations, and unrealistic ideas about a blended family. The battleground can exist in many places: between spouses and ex-spouses, between children from the different marriages, between step-parents and children, and sometimes between the different grandparents. Children face the most disruption and disorientation in these kinds of situations. They haven't asked for this disruption and usually don't have much say in the establishment of a new "family."

It should be a huge red flag if your partner does not assume full emotional, financial, or geographical responsibility for being a parent. If the children are neglected in this way and fail to be a priority, your partner undoubtedly has issues of immaturity and irresponsibility. Will you really respect a partner who slinks away and avoids or excuses him or herself from being a father or mother?

Spencer and Sage were a mismatch from the start. Sage had over $50 000 in credit card debt, while Spencer was very frugal; he was a warehouse loader with a passion for motorcycles, while she was a professional nurse who refused to ride on one. Sage was active in her church community, while Spencer was an atheist, but he didn't resist her attending church as it allowed him time to meet with his friends for motorcycle outings. Plus, their parents didn't approve of the marriage. After eleven years, their differences had become even more profound and they agreed to separate. They had two children: Rob, age ten, and Robin, age eight.

When I met Spencer in my clinical practice, he had been divorced for a year and brought his new partner, Brenda, to the session. Spencer wanted to move to another city—one with a larger motorcycling community—but Brenda was unsure.

I asked Spencer, "What are your plans for the future?"

"Well," Spencer started, "I'd like to head south with Brenda, move out of Canada and into the United States. They have way more motorcycle groups and events down there, and I've finally found someone who loves motorcycles like I do." He looked at his new partner. "Brenda's a great woman, loves bikes. We met online through a bike group. But we're having lots of arguments about moving. She doesn't think I'm doing the right thing moving away from my kids, even though I'll be paying child support."

"And what do you believe is required of you as a father at this time?" I asked.

"The kids spend a lot of time with their friends now, so they don't really need much from me. They can come and visit me during summer holidays. I'll always be available to them as their dad. They can call me whenever; I'll give them a phone card."

Brenda looked concerned. "They do spend a lot of time with their friends," she said, "but you can't have the same influence as their dad if you live in another country, eight hours away. I think you're shirking your responsibilities as a dad and that worries me about you."

Instead of responding to Brenda, Spencer turned to me. "What do you think, Dr. Wright? Is it a good plan?"

Spencer's casual attitude towards his parenting responsibilities surprised me. When I asked him about his experiences with his own father and what it means to be a good father, I began to understand his parenting behaviours.

Spencer had a sad story. Both his parents were killed in a tragic car accident when he was twelve years old. Close friends of his parents adopted him and his ten-year-old sister. The friends were a childless couple who were very laissez-faire, had no parenting experience, and didn't provide much parental guidance. By the time he was sixteen, he left the home and had been on his own ever since. Consequently, Spencer had not witnessed or experienced devoted or committed parents. The adults in his early life had loved him but lacked parenting skills. He now thought it was acceptable to leave children at a critical time in their lives. I offered him a straightforward answer to his question.

"Unfortunately, you didn't receive adequate parenting, even though you did have adults in your life who loved you. Now you must learn how to be a good father from other men, books, parenting courses, and your own wisdom. That can only be done by being present, available, and in the same town as your children. Living somewhere else is not an option until the children are out of the parental home. Otherwise, you're continuing the same legacy of scanty child-rearing that you experienced as a child, and I'm sure that's not a legacy you want to continue."

I was very heartened to see how Spencer immediately took my words to heart. "I needed to hear this. You're right. I didn't have devoted and committed parents, and I don't want my kids to live without their parents close by and fully involved."

Brenda was pleased with his response but somewhat annoyed too. "I'm glad you agree with Dr. Wright's advice, but I've been telling you that all along. And I want you to know that I would not have moved with you to the States. I wouldn't have respected you for leaving your children at such a young age."

Spencer opened his eyes wide. "That's the first time you ever said that! Well, I'm here and not going anywhere. In fact, I'd like to take my kids out for dinner tonight. Wanna come, Brenda?"

In my view, Brenda was a wise and compassionate woman. She had already determined that if Spencer was willing to leave his children for more motorcycling opportunities, he would not have been a suitable candidate for marriage.

This couple continued to date and eventually married. Brenda became an excellent step-parent to Spencer's children, and they wrote me a thank-you note for being so forthcoming and frank with them about Spencer's parenting responsibilities.

Conclusion

We all have those little voices in the back of our minds. They whisper on the first date that the way he stared down that other guy in the room wasn't so much romantic as possessive. They create that niggling feeling in response to her cavalier attitude about not seeing her son. They ring the alarm bell over four glasses of wine on a casual first dinner.

Those little voices shouldn't be ignored if you intend to continue on into a serious relationship. If it's marriage on the line, listen up! Play a few rounds of the "What if?" game and see how you like the answers. What if you marry an alcoholic? What if the drinking escalates? What if that addiction drains your finances? What if you have children? Will they have to see their parent drunk every day? How will you feel in that relationship?

Will a partner you met on vacation be able to handle a simple dinner party at your home with friends? What if that's not enough excitement for him or her? What if the concept of simply being home isn't what they want? Will that relationship, that marriage, provide you with a lifetime of happiness?

What if you marry? Will you adopt his children into your life? Will you make a good step-parent? Will having his children, and his ex-wife, in your life make you happy, while providing the whole family unit with the support it requires?

These are big questions. Bigger than the questions most people ask themselves when buying a dress, taking a job, or planning a honeymoon. Yet they could be the most important questions of your life.

Chapter 2

Risky Situations

There are many happy matches, it is true . .
. but what sensible bachelor, rejoicing in his
freedom and years of discretion, will run the
tremendous risk?

—Mark Twain

Don't Get Married
. . . If either of your parents are opposed to your partner.

Some couples like to cling to a romantic notion that they don't need their parents' approval. If one or both sets of parents oppose your partner, it will be just that—opposition. Couples quickly learn that being estranged from their parents, regardless of how justified they once felt, brings unnecessary hurt and suffering to all. Being alienated from parents because of a marital partner invites some of the deepest angst for newlywed couples. They are living a paradoxical life of a committed marriage, while being separated from their family of origin.

Regardless of age, couples who marry desire the support, approval, and blessing of their parents (and children) upon their choice of a mate. As one newlywed woman said to me: "My parents not supporting me in my marriage left me with a haunting thought of what if they're right? What if I shouldn't have married my husband?" Married couples need, and benefit from, the support of their original families. The more family and friends who sanction the union of the couple, the greater the opportunity for deepening their bond.

I have met couples over the years where a difference in religion, ethnic background, class, sexual orientation, and even their child's partner's occupation have resulted in the parents' opposition to the couple marrying. Some of these couples proceeded with their marriages regardless, claiming their parents to be narrow-minded, rigid, old-fashioned, and/or racist. The more that couples dig in their heels and refuse to attempt to understand or appreciate their parents' point of view, the more distance they create and the longer it takes to heal and reunite.

It's not always your fault, though. Sometimes, it IS the parents who are unable to yield or accept their child's choice of partner because of shame or embarrassment amongst other family members, or their cultural or religious community. Other parents have simply lived vicariously through their children and cannot embrace that their children's dreams of an ideal partner may not be their dreams. Sometimes, the couple has to separate themselves from their parents if there are issues of addictions, abuse, or unhealthy boundaries. In cases like these, time and space can be great healers. The arrival of grandchildren can also be a great healer—but not always.

Abdul was a shy and handsome twenty-two-year-old Arab man whose parents had emigrated from Lebanon when he was five. At university, he met a beautiful, outgoing Caucasian woman named Shannon, who was five years his elder. They were both engineering students and enjoyed studying together. At first, their attraction was cerebral, but soon the intellectual prowess gave way to romantic ties. To save money, the two decided to live together, but Abdul was reluctant to share his newfound love with his widowed mother (his father had passed away two years previously). He assumed she'd hate the idea of him shacking up with a "white girl." He was terrified of her reaction.

Shannon, however, readily told her parents, and they were eager to meet this young man she had told them so much about. The ethnic and religious differences between the two did not bother them, and neither did their cohabitation. They supported the union wholeheartedly.

Seeing this positive reaction from Shannon's parents, Abdul finally worked up his courage and phoned his mother. As he broke the news, she began wailing into the receiver, utterly distraught. Her reaction was even worse than he'd imagined. She wouldn't have minded so much if he had moved in with a Muslim girl. The thought that her eldest son would love and marry outside of their faith was unbearable. She still had two young, impressionable daughters at home; what would they think of their big brother now?

His mother's reaction horrified Abdul, and he took solace in his girlfriend's family. He rarely went home for visits and instead spent long weekends and vacations with Shannon's family. She told him that his mother would "come around" when they married. Wishful thinking. She did not attend their wedding, and Abdul and his mother didn't speak for the next two years. During that time, Abdul suffered periods of depression and anxiety. He sometimes withdrew from Shannon and even slept at the office on occasion. When I met this couple, they were expecting their first child.

Abdul sat motionless and almost speechless while his wife poured out her disdain and upset for Abdul's mother and how she had influenced their marriage.

"Do you believe that Abdul's recurring depressions could be related to being estranged from his mother?" I asked Shannon.

"Sometimes I think that, but then I think if he's going to let her rule him to the point of being depressed, I should never have married him."

"Perhaps you're right," I said. Shannon blinked at me, stunned.

Abdul suddenly sat up in his chair. "I never felt good about marrying without my mother present," he said. "My wedding day was the happiest and saddest day of my life." Shannon began to cry.

"Do you still feel that your marriage is the happiest and saddest part of your life?" I passed Shannon a tissue.

"Yes."

Shannon cried more intensely and said, "Then why don't you go back to your mother?"

"You might be on to something there, Shannon," I said. "Perhaps that's exactly what needs to happen, to reconnect with his mother, but that doesn't necessarily have to mean the end of your marriage."

We were able to discuss how no contact with his mother had caused a piece of Abdul's heart to constantly hurt. Then I asked, "What can you both do now to heal this sorrow in a way that will also heal your marriage?" Both being very bright, they knew they had to solve this rift with Abdul's mother. He said that he wanted his children to know their grandmother.

The first big step was for Abdul to call his mother. He was shocked how cold and uncaring she was. He had hoped she'd be pleased to hear from him, but she wasn't as ready to reconcile as he was. Abdul's rejection had hurt her deeply as well as his choice to marry without her blessing. It took many calls and visits to slowly begin to soften the deep wounds on all sides. Healing would take much longer.

When Shannon went into labour, one of the first phone calls Abdul made was to his mother. She arrived at the hospital just in time to meet her grandson. As she held him for the first time, she looked to Shannon and said, "My son has wasted so much time and aged me so, but I do not want to deprive myself of time with my grandson."

Although this story seems to have a happy ending, most couples are not as lucky. In my practice, I've learned that it takes many years to heal from a family's antagonism. Some never do. My advice is simple: If your family values are deeply rooted, marry within your own faith and ethnic community. When you are well aware of the expectations, hopes, dreams, and sometimes even requirements of your parents, then going against such core beliefs will only provide you with imminent conflict.

If these issues are NOT important to your family of origin, then feel free to explore the possibility of marrying into different faiths, ethnic backgrounds, and cultures. Each of us writes our own family story, and it starts with the partners we choose. For your story to be a happy one, fill it with a large cast of supportive characters from all sides who understand and agree on a set of core values.

. . . *If either of you are separated but not yet divorced.*

When a couple separates, things can get messy. Whatever their intentions—to divorce or reconcile—the situation is complicated. Recent studies indicate that after five years of separation or divorce, couples often wished they had not parted. Why would you get involved with someone who's dealing with that? The residue of the previous marriage will inevitably be dragged into yours.

Being legally divorced isn't the same as being emotionally divorced. When someone is not emotionally divorced, a third person exists in the new relationship. This third person can interfere at many levels, from preventing your partner from being fully engaged or committed to your new relationship, to ongoing conversations about the awful deeds and shortcomings of their ex. Doesn't that sound like a fun date?

Throw some kids into the mix and your life is going to get even more complicated. Custody and financial issues, especially with children, are often undecided and twisted during separation. Separation is a foggy, grey period of time, when all the details of the couple's previous life together have to be reorganized. It's emotional chaos. Through plenty of negotiation, hopefully a semblance of order begins to emerge through the development of a divorce agreement. Actual divorce frequently brings greater clarity to both parties—especially if they are emotionally mature enough to realize the benefits of transparency, collaboration, and cooperation for their children.

Jumping into the middle of a separation, before the dust settles, is lunacy. You can't expect your new relationship to take priority when your partner is still emotionally and financially involved with a spouse. You can't expect that a partner who's trying to shut down or let go of their emotions in one area of their life will be able to open to you in another.

If you or your partner are separated but not divorced, neither of you are good candidates for marriage. More specifically, you are simply not available to marry.

What if you meet someone who IS legally divorced? How do you know if they are emotionally divorced? Simple. Just ask the following litmus test question: "How do you understand that your marriage didn't work for you and your ex?" If the answer involves blame, anger, and bad-mouthing, then you know that he or she is not emotionally divorced. Stop right there. Go no further. This is not a candidate for a current relationship, let alone marriage.

On the other hand, if your potential dating partner says something like, "Well, we both made mistakes" or "we couldn't solve our problems together," you can rest assured that this is the kind of emotionally mature person you might want to get to know better.

Ryan arrived at my office thirty minutes ahead of his partner, Avery, for their first counselling session. This in itself was interesting. Usually, the women are the most eager to show up and talk. When Avery arrived, it was obvious that she was harried and stressed. Her coat was only half buttoned on a very cold day and her hair was flying in all directions. She plopped herself down on an office chair and blurted, "Sorry I'm late. I've just had a horrible phone call with Max."

"And Max is . . . ?"

"My husband. Soon to be ex-husband, that is."

"Oh, I see. You're divorcing." I jotted down a quick note and scanned Ryan's body language. "Before we decide if it's necessary to discuss this phone call, why don't I collect some background information about you two. What are your hopes for this first meeting?"

Ryan was very clear that he had found "the girl of his dreams" and wanted her to speed up the divorce from Max so they could marry.

"I want to get married, too," Avery said, "but there are a lot of details to work out first . . ."

"We've been together two years," Ryan interrupted. "We've lived together for almost all of that and still we're no closer to getting married than we were on our first date."

"Do either of you have children?" I wanted to avoid an argument and focus on sharing.

"No, no kids," Avery said.

After obtaining some initial information and their hopes for the session, I asked Avery the litmus test question.

"Avery, how do you understand that your marriage to Max didn't work out?"

She had an immediate and blaming response. "Because he had an affair with my sister, if you can believe it. But it was short-lived and they're not in a relationship now. I cannot believe to this day that they would betray me like that." I inquired about the relationship with her sister at this moment. She said, "I've forgiven her. It was more my husband's fault. He pushed her, chased her. He told her he had married the wrong sister. She felt so bad about the whole thing. Now we're closer than ever."

Ryan was listening intensely and then said, "We spend too much time talking about Max and what he did and not about us and getting married. When we first met, I listened and supported her, but now I'm tired of this story."

Avery suddenly became furious. "You're *tired* of this story? Well, obviously you don't understand how hurt I've been." She slammed her fist into the chair cushion, her face beet red.

"I've tried to understand, Avery. I have. But you seem as hurt and angry about it as you were two years ago. Can't we move on to *our* relationship?"

Unfortunately, Avery was far from being emotionally or legally divorced.

"Avery," I said, "what would it take for you to begin healing from this deep hurt that happened in your marriage?"

She took a deep breath and offered an incredible insight. "I need Max to say that he *did not* marry the wrong sister. That's more important to me than the affair because if he believes that he married the wrong sister, then our whole marriage was a sham."

This was news to Ryan.

"And if you never hear from Max that he married the right sister, do you think you can go forward with a marriage to Ryan?"

"Perhaps not . . . it wouldn't be fair to Ryan, I guess."

Ryan began to weep. Avery didn't reach out or say anything to comfort him. This further demonstrated that Avery was far from capable of having an intimate relationship with Ryan. She wasn't ready or able to "give her love away."

Following this meeting, I met with Avery individually to help her move forward in her own healing. She invited Max to join her, but he refused. Avery seemed intent on holding on to this one seductive statement that Max made to her sister. She finally admitted that Ryan had been a wonderful sounding board, supportive, and kind, but that she couldn't see herself marrying him.

"Until you are emotionally and legally divorced, the kindest thing you can do is set Ryan free," I said. She agreed and later reported that Ryan took the news better than she thought because of "our counselling session."

The most surprising aspect I learned in individual sessions with Avery was that she still hoped that Max might want to reconcile. I explained to Avery my belief that "rejection is a powerful invitation." She was caught in the trap of needing the person who had rejected and betrayed her to validate her. She found this a useful idea. When I concluded my counselling with Avery, she was beginning to make some progress towards reclaiming herself as a worthy and valued woman.

Conclusion

Getting married is risky enough in this day and age. Don't increase your risk by knowingly stepping into a relationship fraught with extra dangers. Do you really want to spend your days making up for the loss of his mother or fighting the ghost of a soon-to-be ex-husband? When your potential spouse brings this level of baggage into your relationship, you end up being the bellhop.

Every adult comes with their own fair share of issues and experiences, but when they go beyond the norm to stubbornly cling to negative influences, you might have to admit defeat. If your future husband or wife can't see that they need to deal with their parents or their exes before they make their vows to you, they are not going to be the perfect match. Marriage shouldn't be entered into blindly—open your eyes and see clearly the obstacles in your way.

Chapter 3

Goofy Beliefs

By all means, marry. If you get a good wife, you'll become happy; if you get a bad one, you'll become a philosopher.

—Socrates

Don't Get Married
. . . If either of you have goofy beliefs about where to meet a partner and when to marry.

Most often, goofy or foolish beliefs about relationships can invite poor judgment about how to meet a partner and/or when to marry. We all possess strong personal beliefs about relationships and marriage. When out in the world, we hear the beliefs of our families, friends, professionals, spiritual leaders, celebrities, authors, and bloggers. Some of these confirm our own goofiness, while others disconfirm it. Having goofy beliefs isn't necessarily bad, but *acting* on them can invite years of marital torment or heartache, unless some of the poor premarital judgments can be altered.

One of my roles as a marriage and family therapist is to bring forth the constraining or facilitating beliefs and realities of each partner, so I can more fully understand their behaviour. Our beliefs drive our behaviour, and once I understand those beliefs, I can usually calm my own judgmental ideas. It is paramount to scrutinize all of the constraining (goofy) beliefs that limit relationship solutions. My coauthored book *Beliefs and Illness: A Model for Healing* (2009) offers an in-depth understanding of how beliefs emerge and their role in our lives, as well as a full description of constraining/facilitating beliefs.

Over the years, I have heard some of the most astounding and outrageous beliefs about relationships and marriage. A few times I've nearly fallen off my chair and yelled, "You believe WHAT?" The following two examples of goofy beliefs are definite "fall off your chair" goodies:

1. If I can't find a suitable partner in my own country, then I will go on the Internet and find someone in another country.

I have encountered several couples who met and married this way. It's usually men who go trolling the web for a relationship with a woman in a different country. Cultural and language differences are just the beginning of the many challenges these marital unions face. I know, we've all heard of that one couple who met online from different corners of the globe and they're now happily married. They do exist. But trust me, they are the exception to the rule. Statistics show that these transcontinental hook-ups don't work in the long term.

2. The amount of time that you know someone before marriage is not as important as how much you love him or her.

In my clinical practice, I always ask couples for their dating and courtship history. I am particularly interested in how long they dated before cohabiting and/or marrying. My experience has shown that the shorter the period of dating prior to marriage, the more the couple is shocked and surprised at the challenges and angst in their marriage. A good rule of thumb is to never marry before knowing someone at least twelve months. You need to see them through all the seasons. In the early months of a courtship there is often too much gaga and not enough reason. After twelve months, you've gone through every significant occasion (birthdays, Christmas, Passover, etc.), plus have had enough time for the gaga emotions to subside and good sense to arise. Enjoying the gaga feelings can be wonderful; just don't let them shorten the time to marriage.

There are other goofy beliefs such as "you shouldn't have to work at having a good marriage," or "if I'm not happy, I'll just move on," among others. The two that I have discussed here have become especially common in this world of finding romance during international travel.

Many travellers exploring the world will find themselves involved in a romantic fling in a foreign land. Some backpackers will even end up travelling together for a few weeks or months.

Perhaps not surprisingly, most will return to their own countries, alone. These relationships are usually ones of convenience, rather than sustained romance. When the travelling time is shorter—just a quick two weeks in Hawaii—these trysts tend to be more intense and the lovers more determined to make it last.

Such was the case with Carl, a forty-year-old Canadian, and Natalia, a twenty-seven-year-old Argentinian. They met in Cuba on the second day of their vacation and were inseparable for the remaining eight days. When they left Cuba, both professed their love to each other. They were sexually involved on their first evening together. After returning to their home countries, they engaged in all the modern methods of communicating when living at a distance: email, text, Skype, and even old-fashioned phone calls. Still, they couldn't satisfy their need to be in contact with one another, so Carl arranged for a trip to Argentina one month after they met. But before leaving, Natalia began asking more questions about Carl's personal life and previous relationships.

Up to that point, Carl hadn't disclosed that he'd

had two previous relationships (one a marriage) and that he had an eighteen-year-old daughter. At first, Natalia was upset that he hadn't told her everything sooner. "No, no, 1 wasn't hiding anything," he said in a soothing voice. "1 was simply so in love with you that it never entered my mind." And she bought that. Carl never even questioned if Natalia had a previous marriage, but she spontaneously offered that she had not, nor did she have any children.

Carl travelled to Argentina for ten whirlwind days, meeting Natalia's family and friends. He proposed during this time and Natalia accepted. Natalia's family was ambivalent about Carl and very sad that Natalia would be moving to Canada. They didn't see each other again for three months while Natalia obtained her visa. At the end of three months, Carl spent another quick week in Argentina for their wedding and then both returned to Canada. The total amount of time they had spent together before marriage was twenty-two days. As well as believing that finding love on foreign shores was a good idea, Carl and Natalia both shared the goofy belief that "the amount of time that you know someone before marriage is not as important as how much you love them."

After arriving in Canada, Carl and Natalia faced

immediate challenges. Natalia was dreadfully lonely and missed her family and friends. Carl had returned to work and so they weren't together twenty-four hours a day, like they had been on vacation. His home was in a suburb of his city with no amenities within walking distance. Natalia didn't have a driver's licence and was timid about taking public transportation, so she waited for Carl to go anywhere. She felt terribly isolated and asked Carl where she could meet other South American people in the city. He didn't know, but he told her he preferred that she get to know his friends and befriend his daughter.

I met this couple after they had been married and living in Canada for nine months. Natalia's loneliness and social isolation weren't the biggest concerns that she presented. Their biggest conflict was over Carl not wanting children and Natalia longing to have them. Natalia claimed that during one of Carl's visits to Argentina, he had said, "I don't mind if you get pregnant." Carl denied ever having said that and could not remember discussing children at all. He claimed that if they had discussed children, he would have told her he was content with the daughter he already had.

"I never would have married him if I had known that," Natalia said. "But I love him. I've begged him to change his mind and all he says is no. He says he will never change his mind."

When I explored his reasons for not desiring children, Carl said it was also a financial concern. Natalia had told him that she wanted to return to Argentina at least once a year so that their children could know their Argentinian grandparents.

"I can't afford that," he said. "Airfare for Natalia and the kids all the way there and back. No way. She should just make friends, work, and be satisfied with life here and our marriage. Why can't her family come here to visit?"

Natalia sat, stunned.

The baby impasse had lowered Carl's sexual desire because he was afraid Natalia would stop using birth control. Consequently, they hadn't had sexual relations for the last four months of their nine-month marriage. Natalia wept when discussing this situation and said she didn't want a childless marriage or a sexless one.

It was now time for me to speak the unspeakable and ask the tough questions. "Knowing what you each know now, what would you do differently?"

Natalia immediately said, "I would not let a vacation romance lead to marriage after only twenty-two days of being together."

Carl said, "We never discussed our goals for marriage, like children. What a huge mistake. And everything just moved way too fast."

"So what now?" I asked. "Do you think that your differences are resolvable?" They both cried and said "no." Natalia said that she would be embarrassed to return to Argentina having made this mistake. But Carl suddenly manned up and took full responsibility.

"I'll go with you to Argentina and explain to your parents that it's my fault that we didn't discuss things thoroughly before marriage and that you deserve to have children and be close to your family." Natalia was shocked and cried more at Carl's kind offer.

I commended Carl's willingness to travel with Natalia and assume the greater responsibility for their marriage breakdown. However, both Natalia and Carl took responsibility for their poor decision to rush to the altar. After Carl accompanied Natalia to Argentina, he called me upon his return to Canada. He said it broke his heart to leave Natalia in Argentina, and he was still very much in love with her. More importantly, he realized that if he wouldn't have children with her, it was not loving to have her remain in Canada. I told him I admired his maturity in realizing that real love is sometimes letting another go so that they can fulfill their life's desires. Plus, Carl also came to realize that meeting and falling in love with someone while on an international vacation does not resemble real-life dating and courtship. It starts fast and can end just as quickly.

Conclusion

What's the rush? Whether it's you pushing to get to the altar or your partner, take a moment and ask why. Do you really think that skipping the dating process and marrying the first eligible candidate you find on an international vacation will make your life easier? Spoiler alert, it's not.

Knowing the person you're marrying and getting to know their family gives your relationship the best possible chance at success. Spending time together and living near each other is the only way to make that happen.

Meeting someone from a foreign country and falling head over heels in love on the white sand beaches is the ultimate romantic fantasy to many people. But that's what it is—a fantasy. Once you're faced with the realities of a long, cold winter and a homesick, family-deprived spouse, you'll soon know the difference.

Take a breath. Take your time. Know your future spouse and the pitfalls of international dating before you log onto that website. Visas, culture shock, travel expenses, the loss of family support and friends—not exactly a recipe for the best time of your life.

Chapter 4

Deficit Experiences

The desire to get married is a basic and primal instinct in women. It's followed by another basic and primal instinct: the desire to be single again.

—Nora Ephron

Don't Get Married
. . . *If either of you don't have the basic experiences necessary to maintain a mature relationship.*

What are some important experiences to have prior to marrying? Some might say travelling, finishing college, or having that one big adventure you've always wanted to do solo. These kinds of experiences may or may not make any difference to your eventual marital satisfaction, but there are a handful of must-have experiences that will increase the likelihood of making you a more credible candidate for marriage. I've compiled six of the most relevant and reliable must-haves:

1. Have your own bank account.

Having your own bank account usually means you will have experienced learning to save money and how to spend it. Many parents establish accounts for their children, but it's only when you have taken full control of your bank accounts for spending, saving, and that other real-life experience of paying bills, that you are truly ready for marriage. Money has often been blamed as a cause of divorce, yet this has not been my experience in assisting couples. Rather, I have witnessed that it is the lack of experience in managing money or differences about who is going to be in charge or control of the finances that causes problems. You need to decide early on how your household income will be handled. Is one of you better at money management than the other? Will you handle your accounts jointly? Who will be the primary bill payer? However you decide to handle your finances, you both have to be in agreement.

Learning each other's competencies,

especially in money matters, can save a lot of unnecessary angst about spending and saving. One couple told me that they always consult one another if anything costs more than $25.00, but another couple said they only consult one another about big purchases, like a new car. Values about money can vary dramatically based on your upbringing and attitudes.

If you both want to be involved in decisions about saving, spending, and managing money, then having previous experience with money will help you know your strengths and weaknesses as you try to avoid the potential pitfalls of money management.

2. Have a part- or full-time job.

If your parents were paying attention, you had chores growing up. Household responsibilities like cleaning up after meals, taking out the garbage, or washing the family car are essential beginnings for the development of good work skills. It isn't, however, a substitute for gaining experience working outside the home. Getting to work on time, learning how to work and cooperate with others, having responsibilities at a workplace, obtaining feedback about your work skills, collecting a paycheck, and deciding how to spend or save are all vital experiences prior to marriage.

Not having had a part- or full-time job indicates you are either too young to marry or too immature to know you should have a job. Even the Kardashian children have jobs, in their own way. If you are neither too young nor the child of a celebrity, then you need to put yourself out there in the world and learn what it's like to work for pay. Many of you reading this book have held several part-time jobs while finishing high school and/or college, or you've already finished college/university and now are well into establishing a career. If so, you can happily cross this off your list of deficit experiences. Make sure your potential spouse can say the same.

3. Be at least twenty-five years old with no more than a ten-year age difference between you and your potential spouse.

What age a person is when they marry does matter—a lot! If both partners are teenagers when they marry, it dramatically increases the likelihood of divorce. This makes perfect sense. Teenagers haven't fully matured, experienced personal financial stability, or completed their education. If only one partner is a teenager, the chances of a successful marriage increase only slightly. Do yourself a favour and wait.

If there is more than a ten-year gap between the ages of spouses, their differences expand beyond age to issues of maturity, life experiences, and even philosophies of life. Someone born in the 1990s is bound to have a different world view than someone born in the 1970s. There's just no way around this. You've witnessed different things and experienced more or less. You've seen the world evolve to a greater or lesser extent, loved more or less, and matured differently. This puts one partner in a position of having greater experience than the other.

The larger the age difference, the more likely a couple is to slide into a parent-child relationship rather than standing on equal footing. This imbalance may not be apparent initially, but it will always reveal itself in time.

Why do you need to be twenty-five years old? The drop in the high divorce risk of teen marriage levels off in the early twenties; that is, one doesn't decrease the risk any further by waiting to marry until the late twenties or thirties. Twenty-five or older has become the golden rule.

For those interested in a mathematical formula for when to marry, an Optimal Proposal Age for men has been developed. Just fill in the following mathematical formula:

Choose the oldest age in which you want to get married; for example, 39. Call this number "n." Choose the earliest age in which you'll start to consider women as potential wives; for example, from 20 onwards. Call this number "p." Subtract "p" from "n" (20 - 39) then multiply the result by 0.368. This gives you 6.992, which you now add to your minimum age (20). The result of 27 (rounded up) is your Optimal Proposal Age.

4. Complete high school.

Some statistics just don't lie. Like the one that indicates that those who have not completed high school are more likely to divorce than those who have. Maybe you've been dragging your feet when it comes to getting your diploma, or you're managing to work and make some good cash without it. Whatever your story, whatever your reasons, go to night school and finish. Get that GED! Be on the safe side. Why tempt fate and the statistics?

5. Don't date too few or too many.

We can all cite couples from high school or college who are now happily celebrating their fortieth wedding anniversary, but these virgin couples are not the norm in North American society. Most adults of marrying age have already been in a relationship or two—and that's not a bad thing. Those who have test-driven more than one relationship won't focus so much on whether the other person is a good candidate for marriage but rather if they themselves have the necessary skills to enter into marriage.

Having some real experience in the dating world increases your knowledge about yourself and about how to assess others. When entering into a marriage, being young and naïve could leave you heartbroken and jaded. You need to be ready—really ready—with the necessary life experiences and the necessary relationship and communication skills before you walk down the aisle.

What if you've had numerous relationship experiences? Is there such a thing as too many? Yes! Over the many years that I have been providing consultation and counselling to couples, I have derived that having more than one relationship in your teens and twenties usually provides you with healthy relationship experiences. However, having many relationships in your thirties and forties is a huge red flag! Jumping in and out of relationships at this advanced age could mean many things (poor relationship and/or communication skills, alcohol or drug abuse problems, financial problems), but it usually means that one has definite deficits that need to be addressed. If you or your potential mate hasn't been able to commit within two decades of dating, you have to ask if you'll ever be ready.

Another red flag that I've garnered over the years is when one or both potential partners have cohabited several times. More often it is men who may have cohabited several times, rather than women.

6. Be careful if one of you has never married and one is divorced or widowed.

If you are in a relationship where one of you is divorced and one has never married, then a major deficit in life experience exists: marriage. That deficit will only become problematic if the partner who is divorced has legally but not emotionally divorced. If the divorced person is still blaming and angry towards their former spouse, then they're not emotionally divorced and therefore not ready for another marriage. Equally, if the one who has never married is constantly comparing her or himself to their partner's amazing deceased spouse, then they also don't have the maturity to enter into a marriage.

Conclusion

Grow up before you walk down the aisle, and make sure your spouse does, too! No one wants to be married to a child. Whether you and your mate are equally young or just one of you is, the chances of a successful union are limited. How can you expect to be an emotionally mature husband or wife if you've never balanced your cheque book—or even HAD a cheque book, for that matter.

Marriage is a sacred union in which you and your spouse are meant to grow old together. It's not a place to grow up together. Come into this most meaningful bond on the equal footing of full-blown adulthood.

On life's checklist, these items are fundamental and should be universal:

- ✓ open and manage a bank account
- ✓ get a job
- ✓ finish high school
- ✓ make sure the person you intend to marry has done the same.

To give your marriage a fighting chance, you and your spouse must start off from the same place. If she's in her late thirties and has had twelve relationships in the past ten years, ask yourself (and her) why. Notice the patterns. If he's been married, divorced, and/or widowed, but you have never taken the plunge, be careful. Your life experiences will never be equal.

Part II

Don't Get Married . . . Unless You Are Prepared to Prepare Yourself

Nothing has produced more unhappiness than the concept of the soulmate.

—Frank Pittman

Introduction

Can a person *really* prepare oneself for marriage? Absolutely! Can a *couple* really prepare themselves for marriage? Of course! Will your spouse be your soulmate? Well, first we need to ask if soulmates exist. Unfortunately, the concept of "soulmates" is one of the greatest myths in the world of dating and love. Hollywood and fairy tales have upheld this ideal for ages. Who can possibly live up to the moniker of "soulmate," to be the mirror reflection of another person's deepest needs and desires at all times? To be the perfect, ideal mate every minute of every day? No one could withstand that pressure. It's an unrealistic expectation of your mate.

A more desirable goal would be to find a mate with a soul, someone who possesses compassion, understanding, values, and kindness. But are *you* a person with soul? Do you possess the qualities it takes to make yourself a great, if not at least a good, candidate for marriage? It starts with you. By making sure you're ready for marriage, you will demand the same in your partner. Someone

93

who's confident in their ability to love and sustain a healthy relationship will seek out their equal. *You are the first step to a fortified and secure marriage.*

The best way to ensure that your marriage has an excellent chance to succeed is to prepare yourself. These next three chapters will explain the most important areas to prepare and how to do it.

Chapter 5

Get to Know You, Get to Know All About You . . .

Was it love at first sight? It wasn't then, thirty years ago—but it sure is now.

—Anne Meara

Don't Get Married
. . . Unless you and your partner are prepared to REALLY get to know each other.

Getting to know someone deeply after thirty years of marriage, as Anne Meara suggests, makes love grow deeper—so much so that it can feel as strongly as "love at first sight." In the classic movie *The King and I*, Rodgers and Hammerstein wrote a song called "Getting to Know You," with the famous lyrics "Getting to know you, getting to know all about you, getting to like you, getting to hope you like me." So how best can young (and old) couples come to know one another? Through good old-fashioned dating, or "courting" as we used to say. Dating is different from "hooking up," although it is an ambiguous term ranging from casual, intermittent dating to casual sex. There is no substitute for traditional dating. Try as we might to compress our time and rush our decisions, there's simply nothing better when searching for a mate than getting to know them. You might be able to rush love, but you can't rush a happy marriage.

For many single twenty-, thirty-, or forty-somethings, the idea of dating has become a chore—the last item on a long to-do list—and some even consider it obsolete. Many will say that they are too busy or too exhausted after studying or working all day to find someone to date. Or they might postpone this "chore" in order to finish their education and embark on their careers. Dating now feels like another full-time job. Many don't want a relationship that involves a slow progression from the initial meeting to substantial, frequent, and intense "getting to know you" dating. Unfortunately, when they are ready for a true romantic relationship, they don't know how to find it and lack the skills for getting to know someone.

If they do find someone they'd like to know better, many will resort to social media for shortcuts. Instead of spending time together and, brace yourself, *talking*, they will sit alone at their respective computers stalking Facebook pages, trading emails and emoticons, and assuming that a carefully crafted IM is the same as a conversation.

Traditional dating is experiencing a seismic shift. The Internet has changed how we meet and interact. It offers the convenience of online dating. Sure, this can be handy for initially meeting someone, but traditional dating needs to take over after that.

Efficiency is held up as an icon in the office, but romance is based on leisure time, not efficiency. Dating used to be a slow progression from finding someone to marry to marriage itself, a passage to adulthood. Now, dating has been replaced by sequential casual relationships.

Ironically, there is at the same time an explosion of interest in dating and relationships. There are numerous advice columns and books on dating, courses on relationships, and movies geared towards finding romance. Most recently, popular reality dating shows such as "The Bachelor" and "The Bachelorette" have promoted the ridiculous notion that a marriage partner can be found amongst a group of women or men with just a few dates and millions watching.

If the ritual of dating has changed, then how do couples come to know one another? Unfortunately, living together has become the norm.

Cautions about Cohabitation

As part of our fast-paced society, cohabitation has become a recognized relationship status, even replacing traditional dating and marriage. It seems like the perfect answer to our oh-so-busy lives. Get rid of courtship, dating, and marriage, and replace all three with the one easy step of shacking up (as my father still calls it). After a few casual encounters, many couples decide to live together as part of their assessment of their compatibility for marriage.

The myth here is that couples believe they can really get to know one another this way. Many couples believe that "living together" is an essential prerequisite to marriage. However, research shows that living together does not determine a satisfying or successful marriage, and it doesn't provide the necessary data to prepare for marriage. "Living together" is just that . . . living together.

It seems that women who choose to live with their partner have usually decided that he is "the one;" men who live with their partner have not. Men move in with their partners to make that determination. Consequently, this puts the relationship on an uneven keel, with one partner already having decided that marriage is the desirable outcome of living together and one being uncertain. A pattern evolves where men often become pressured to decide and then find themselves "sliding into marriage," rather than "deciding to marry," as Scott Stanley so aptly suggests in his article "Sliding Versus Deciding: Inertia and the Premarital Cohabitation Effect" (2006).

A classic example of this pattern of "women deciding and men sliding (or not) into marriage" was evident with Andrew and Patrice. When I met this couple, they had been living together for two years. Patrice was exasperated waiting for Andrew to make a decision about marriage. I asked them, "What were your expectations about marriage when you moved in together?"

Patrice was quick to respond. "I always thought we were getting married. I would never have moved in with him if I had known that two years later we would still be living together."

Andrew's understanding was quite different and exemplifies the current gender differences often found in couples who cohabitate. He hesitantly said, "I thought *maybe* we might get married. But I'm happy with the way things are right now and don't see any rush."

"Rush ... are you serious? We've been together for two years, that's hardly rushing. When are you going to make a decision? That's what I keep asking him."

Andrew was not moved by her anguish and did not say or do anything to comfort her. At that moment, I thought it best to share that in my experience of counselling couples, the longer it takes to make a decision about marriage, the more unlikely it is that marriage will happen. Just as I concluded my comment, Andrew jumped in and said, "I think if I'm really honest, I'm not the marrying kind."

Patrice began to weep. "I feel like a fool. I think I've known for a year now that we weren't going to marry, but I kept hoping you would come around."

Sadly, but thankfully for Patrice, this couple separated within a week. She was now able to move on in her life without playing the "waiting for a proposal game" that many women endure. It was brave of Andrew to finally admit that he was not "the marrying kind" at that time in his life, or perhaps not with Patrice. Andrew could have saved a lot of angst for Patrice if he had declared himself more openly when they first broached the idea of living together.

The most interesting statistics from this new data show that a successful marriage can arise out of a cohabitating couple when they are engaged prior to living together. Unfortunately, the statistics of divorce are beginning to indicate that there is more divorce among couples who have lived together prior to marriage than those who did not. Children born to couples who live together have about twice the risk of seeing their parents split than those with married biological parents.

One study titled "Cohabiting and Marriage During Young Men's Career Development Process" (2003) revealed that a man is more likely to live with a woman outside marriage if he is financially unstable. It suggests that the reason more Americans in recent decades have been living together is that men are considering their employment stability and future economic prospects before deciding whether to marry.

"I am not saying that people are so materialistic," said Valerie Oppenheimer, author of the study and a sociologist at UCLA. "What I am really talking about is uncertainly—uncertainty about what sort of person they are and what the future might be. These men came of age during a period of major changes in American society, in which public attitudes became more accepting of premarital sex."

The study says that for many young men, living with a woman outside of marriage serves as a "fall-back strategy" for those who have yet to establish a career.

Men and women both benefit emotionally from being together, whether they're married or cohabitating, and they both have problems after a split—but with some surprising differences. Cohabitating seems to be beneficial to men's mental health and less beneficial to women's mental health.

The difference between men and women in their reaction to cohabitation may be due to women wanting more security in a relationship. In cohabitating, there isn't as much security as marriage implies.

Overall, single women still tend to be better at looking after themselves than single men. Men tend to rely on one person, usually their spouse, while women tend to have a wider circle of friends and a broader social network.

Couples often move in together too quickly, without having talked about their hopes and expectations of living together. Women generally have a more defined idea that this is the interim step between dating and marriage. For men, it is not part of the continuum of the relationship but rather for convenience—financially, socially, and sexually. From the research about dating patterns and cohabitation, it seems that women who are going to cohabitate will spare themselves much emotional suffering if they are at least engaged first. That way, both partners are clear about the fact that a marriage will occur. Eventually.

Most importantly, though, statistics and stories of young couples indicate that a renaissance of dating needs to occur as the most helpful tool for couples getting to know one another. Dating provides a great context for experiencing each other in a variety of settings, with others and by themselves. It allows you to get to know one another without the pressure of paying bills, doing household chores, or negotiating computer time. It should evolve over time, starting with just the two of you and growing to include meeting each other's friends and family. Marriage, when successful, isn't just about two people. It's about root families merging and blossoming and the inclusion of each other's friends into your social network (not Facebook, your real-life social network!).

A generation ago, dating took place in the context of a community. You had family around who knew both of you and your respective families. Now, singles, who have concentrated on furthering educations and advancing careers, live in a more anonymous and mobile society. Old friends and family are not around as much to offer insight and guidance. Courtship, once a family-inclusive affair, has become a solo hunt.

Even at college, which used to be a place to practice meeting suitable mates while preparing for the future, is no longer viewed as such. Western campuses are witnessing the demise in the practice of dating. Girls, in particular, in colleges and universities now believe that having a boyfriend is too time-consuming. Rather than the true intimacy of a real relationship, they're opting more often for friends-with-benefits.

Conclusion

In the now infamous words of Beyoncé, "Put a ring on it!" If marriage is your ultimate goal, don't jump the steps in getting there. Date. Court. Fall in love. Get ENGAGED. Be clear about your intentions and your partner's intentions before you start packing your bags and buying new dishes.

I believe that getting to know one another is one of the most important preparations for marriage and it cannot be rushed. Dating needs to be resurrected, revered, and reinstituted as the primary method of getting to know one another as potential marriage partners.

So go on, date! Have fun and create memories together. It's a habit that will serve you well as you decide whether or not to marry this person and, if you do, throughout your marriage.

Chapter 6

Gain Some Relationship and Communication Skills

The most important marriage skill is listening to your partner in a way that they can't possibly doubt that you love them.

—Diane Sollee

The key to our success in marriage is very simple. Within minutes after every fight, I say, "I'm sorry."

—Jefferson Machamer

Don't Get Married
. . . *Unless you and your partner are prepared to understand each other.*

To really learn relationship and communication skills, memorize John Gray's advice (author of the well-known book *Men Are from Mars, Women*

Are from Venus [1992]): Women want to feel cared about, understood, and respected; men want to feel trusted, accepted, and appreciated. If we embrace these basic emotional needs of men and women, then our relationship and communication skills must focus on how to meet these needs. The following are what I believe to be the seven most important communication and relationship skills to learn in order to prepare for marriage.

1. Learn what to say (and how to listen).

When it comes to communication, men and women have different skills and different needs. Men need to hear they've done a good job, so remember to compliment him for the things he does (even if he doesn't do them that well). Women need to feel their man is listening. Men should practice the following mantra . . .

Just listen, don't give advice.

Just listen, don't give advice.

Just listen, don't give advice.

This is one of the most important, if not the most important, communication skills that both men and women need to learn: Listen FIRST! Then ask if your partner would like advice, an opinion, or a recommendation. Men are often shocked to learn that women often want none of the above.

Avoid data dumps. Couples need to learn what kind of content and stories to share. For example, Michiko meets her partner, Nori, at a restaurant after work and begins telling him the twelve things she did that day. At about item number eight, Nori is ready to scream. Don't share details of the day with your partner; it's like a bad news broadcast. Instead, share one of the day's happenings that had a real emotional impact. Talk about how you reacted and explore why you reacted that way. Have a conversation about something important rather than focusing on the minutiae.

2.   **Learn how to take an interest and to be interesting.**

This is a core relationship skill! It will vary from time to time—one person may take more of an interest in the other and share less about him or herself or vice versa—but overall it should be fairly balanced. Nothing can be more relationship depleting than being with someone who only talks about him or herself and doesn't have the skills or interest to turn the conversation around and ask about the other. To be curious about others is not only respectful, but it also indicates an openness to learn from and be fully engaged with others. In most human interactions, more attention is often paid to the person who talks the most. Sometimes talkative people are entertaining and interesting, but it can become irritating and annoying if there isn't mutual interest.

Conversely, the quiet person who is often referred to as a "good listener" and/or does not offer any spontaneous stories or self-disclosure has an equally significant cause for concern and needs to improve their relationship skills. Being a good listener is an important relationship skill but not to the exclusion of never or rarely sharing about themselves. Not sharing about oneself or responding to what others are sharing leaves the "talker" wondering what the other person thinks and feels, or even who they are. Only listening is not being fully engaged in a relationship.

As one husband told me in couples therapy, "My wife complains that I talk all the time, but she never talks and it makes me anxious. I never know what she's thinking or feeling 'cause she never talks about herself. Her mother says that's because she's so polite and interested in others, but no one really gets to know my wife, not even me. When we first dated, I fell into the same hole and thought, what a great woman, so interested in others. But after ten years, I feel like I'm living with a rock."

After I had an opportunity to meet with his wife individually, I learned that she had been emotionally and physically abused as a child and that being quiet and only listening to others reduced the possibility of further hurt. This way of relating stuck, and she carried it into her marriage and adult friendships. She had erased herself as a person with valid ideas, beliefs, and experiences. This way of relating is very hard to overcome, but we chipped away at it, and she began sharing one story about herself each day with her husband. Stories eventually lead to feelings, and then feelings lead to being more in touch with her emotions. You can imagine that as this woman began sharing herself with her husband, she felt more valued and validated as a person, which had been missing for far too long in her marriage and in her life. She finally had a voice in her significant relationships.

Each of us has a responsibility in all our relationships, but especially in marriage, that all have sufficient air and listening time. We know that women tend to use more words in a day than men do, but opportunities for being interesting and taking an interest can still take place regardless of the word count. Every once in a while, ask yourself, "Would I want to have dinner with me?" If the answer is no—I talk too much and tend to ramble on regardless of how many times my dinner date yawns—then you have some work to do. Or if the answer is "I mostly listen and rarely share anything about myself," then you are also not an ideal dinner date. You need to learn that taking an interest in others and being interesting through self-disclosure and storytelling about one's life makes for balanced and stimulating relationships.

3. **Be respectful and kind, both publicly and privately.**

Other than physically or emotionally cheating on your partner, there is no greater pain one can inflict than shaming your partner or spouse in public. When you're out in the world, remember that you want to treat your partner with the utmost respect. Don't put them down. This is a good rule in general but even more so when you're speaking about them to other people.

To shame your date in public leaves him or her feeling embarrassed, beaten, and vulnerable. And it also leaves them ashamed and embarrassed about *you*. If one can speak harshly and disrespectfully to their partner in public, then you can be confident it will be ten times more disrespectful in private. This is more than being rude or discourteous. This is emotional abuse. It includes problem behaviours such as name-calling (idiot, jerk, loser, no-good), unflattering nicknames, insulting labels, and sarcasm.

Another form of emotional abuse is demeaning statements, everything from trivializing the effort put into preparing a dinner for friends or completing a major paper for a course. Fault-finding or criticism chips away at a person's sense of worth. It's not done out of a genuine regard to help someone be a better person, as some claim, but to elevate the critic and deflect from their own insecurities.

Sometimes emotional abuse takes the form of intimidation. Venting anger through harsh words, shouting, stomping, and/or throwing or breaking things are abusive actions. Learn to recognize them. More importantly, learn to never accept them.

One of the worst forms of emotional abuse is when an individual seeks to limit his or her partner's interaction. Isolation from the outside world breeds dependency on the abuser. This most insidious tactic creeps into relationships slowly, gradually cutting you off from family, friends, and any possible support. It can include such things as withholding information or affection.

If you experience even one of these negative behaviours in your "getting to know you" dating experiences or even after moving in together, recognize it immediately as a HUGE red flag! Your partner needs to do some serious work. If you are the one exhibiting these kinds of behaviours,

STOP! Recognize that you have work to do to learn how to behave with respect, kindness, and compassion towards others and yourself.

Set the bar high when it comes to how you wish to be treated and how you treat your partner. The most successful couples are those who, even in courtship, refuse to accept hurtful behaviour from one another. The lower the level of tolerance for bad behaviour at the start of a relationship, the happier the couple is down the road. Stand firm and practice statements such as "I feel embarrassed when you talk to me like that in front of our friends. Could we talk in private if you are upset with me?" Or "When you criticize me, I don't feel close to you." Then wait, a minute, a day, a week, and see if there is an apology, an understanding, or an effort to make a change in behaviour. If none of these occur, then this person needs to work on his or her relationship and communication skills and is NOT a candidate for marriage.

I have worked with many couples considering marriage (and even after marriage) where these abusive behaviours were turned around, eliminated, and eventually forgiven. But, oh, it is hard work. New skills need to be learned, and the biggest challenge is learning compassion for others and the effect of one's behaviour upon another. It can happen IF an individual is willing to learn some communication skills, empathy, and compassion in order to function with less ego and control in relationships.

4. **Learn to soothe yourself and your partner.**

When your partner is having trouble coping— with the world or with you—don't shout, don't pout, don't run away. Just turn to your partner and lovingly ask, "Dear, what do you need from me right now?" This skill is all about learning how to soothe your partner. Then do what he or she requests. This will lessen his or her troubles and frustrations. This is also part of learning what works and what doesn't when a partner offers to soothe.

Plus YOU must learn how to self-soothe. Learn what works for you to manage your own personal stress, so that you don't bring anger, frustration, and hurt from work, other relationships, or other situations unnecessarily into your courtship relationship. Take care of yourself through rest, leisure, exercise, and pleasant personal diversions. These are, of course, very general suggestions of how to self-soothe. Each of us needs to learn what specific self-soothing techniques work for us. For one person it may be a quiet hour reading, for another it could be having a green tea latte at Starbucks, and for another going for a run. Many are now turning to meditation and/or spiritual practices. This will allow you to give more energy to your relationship, instead of being a source of strain and worry.

What happens when we don't learn self-soothing techniques? Well, the obvious happens. We blame our partner for our stress and how we're feeling, and become irritable and impatient. If non-soothing efforts continue for months or worse yet, years, then more dramatic solutions are often sought, such as excessive drinking or pornography. Self-soothing techniques will evolve and change over a lifetime, but not the need for them.

5. **Learn how to disagree, agreeably.**

Conflict is good. Conflict shows engagement. Conflict gives couples a chance to clarify their own thoughts and emotions. If not confronted, minor irritations will grow and escalate. The number one predictor of divorce is the habitual avoidance of conflict. It is better to learn how to deal directly with conflict than to avoid it. However, the process should be respectful and courteous. This is where the big challenge begins. How DOES one deal with conflict and differences in a loving, kind manner?

First, pick your battles. Don't argue about every little thing that happens: save it for the issues that are really important (see the forty-eight-hour principle in Part III). Your partner won't tune out and you won't turn into a nag.

If something is really important and needs to be brought up, John Gottman suggests softening your "start up" in his book *Seven Principles for Making Marriages Work* (2000). Instead of throwing a tantrum or yelling, try approaching the issue in a softer manner. You can complain, but don't blame. "I feel as though . . ." or "I'm having trouble understanding ____. Can you help

118

me with this?" You're much more likely to get the positive response you're looking for if you start softly. Arguments flare because spouses escalate the conflict from the get-go and keep trying to one-up each other, hurt for hurt.

Second, take a break. If an argument gets too heated, take a twenty-minute break and agree to approach the topic again when you are both calm. This is especially important for men as anger dissipates more slowly physiologically in men than it does in women. When men are angry, blood pressure, pulse, and respirations tend to level off slowly. This is often one of the reasons that men try to avoid conflict. Angry feelings are physically uncomfortable for them, so it's important that men learn to engage in conflict and disagreements, without making their blood pressure skyrocket.

Most importantly, focus on being kind and not on being right. It's easy to spend time showing your partner that you're right. By focusing on being kind, you'll argue less and enjoy each other more.

As the argument draws to a close, once you've said what needed to be said and your partner has heard you, be quick to apologize and forgive. Events will happen that are truly unfortunate, neglectful, mean-spirited, selfish, and just plain wrong. Every relationship will have its emotional wounds and traumas. You have to develop an attitude of resolving these issues quickly. Not forgiving is not an option if you want that love to continue.

6. Learn how to give and be giving.

Real giving is when we give to our spouses what's important to *them*, whether we understand it, like it, agree with it, or don't agree with it. This is great advice from Michele Weiner-Davis, author of *Divorce Busting* (1992). But individuals need to learn this skill well before marriage. For some people, being giving is a natural state of being. For others, it is a learned behaviour; it requires much practice before and during marriage. Learn to recognize your giving-less moments; when you feel justified to not do as much for your partner and when you worry if the other person is giving as much as you. In seeing these not-so-flattering tendencies in ourselves, we can begin to correct them. Change your focus from trying to give the least you can to trying to give the most you can. This isn't about giving more than your partner. Keeping score doesn't build trust and goodwill; it only ensures that one of you is the loser. Challenge yourself to find ways to increase your own giving nature.

7. **Learn different styles of sharing and bonding.**

Whether you are in a new relationship or assessing your current relationship, remember that there are huge gender differences between the ways men and women share and connect. This is not a bad thing. It isn't something to criticize, make fun of, or demean. It's just different and foundational to our DNA. Women tend to bond with one another through conversation and exchanging stories and deeply personal feelings. Men, on the other hand, can experience deep bonding and feel close to other men or you through action—watching hockey playoffs together, painting the home office together, or shopping for a new iPhone together. They don't need to be vulnerable or share deeply to feel a significant bond. Although women may never understand how this is possible, it's often not necessary for deep feelings to be shared to feel a significant bond. It is just as valid for men to connect through activities as it is for women to connect through conversation about their feelings and relationships.

What does this mean for bonding and sharing in a new relationship? It means that you shouldn't try to convert your man into talking with you like your girlfriends, and men shouldn't expect their new partner to watch every football game or play his favourite computer game with him. But we CAN be willing to watch football, maybe the Super Bowl, once in a while, and men CAN learn to occasionally invite a conversation of "so tell me how you're doing." We can see each other's strengths and limitations and learn to bend.

Conclusion

Communication, sharing, and bonding are the foundations of any successful marriage. We all want to be heard and to share experiences—and that includes your spouse. Take the time to learn precisely what your husband or wife needs from you. Communicate your own needs in a way they can hear.

It may sound simple, almost too simple, but it really is the key. Learn to listen and how to be heard; be kind, especially when you're arguing; learn to soothe yourself and your partner. If home isn't a place where you find solace, you'll look for it elsewhere, and so will your spouse. Understand that disagreeing is natural, normal, and often necessary, but it doesn't mean you have to "fight" all the time. Know when to back away, when to take a break, and when to soldier through. Be giving and learn how to receive. And be interesting to and interested in your spouse. Marriage is, hopefully, a long road. Make sure you're the best possible companion for the journey.

Chapter 7

Obtain Premarital or Marriage Education and/or Premarital Counselling

Marriage education workshops can make a real difference in helping married couples stay together and in encouraging unmarried couples who are living together to form a more lasting bond.

—Barack Obama, The Audacity of Hope, 2006, p.334

Don't Get Married
. . . Unless you and your partner are prepared to learn together.

There are a plethora of courses available these days on everything from how to cook like Jamie Oliver, to how to meditate, to how to train for a marathon. In today's information age, we're constantly learning new skills and acquiring new knowledge on a vast list of interests and hobbies. We're becoming better athletes, better shoppers, better pet owners, but do we ever learn to be better spouses? Surprisingly (or not), very few of today's couples ever think about taking a course on marriage before they marry. Somehow we've been conditioned to believe that marriage is just something we'll automatically know how to do. We all know the dismal statistics on modern divorce rates, yet we still don't think a lesson or two is needed. We need to change our collective thinking here.

This chapter is to encourage you, no, to persuade, cajole, and convince you of the importance of taking a marital education course. For couples about to marry, a marriage education course needs to become a compulsory part of preparing for marriage. I recommend to every couple I meet who have a desire to marry to enroll in a course.

Diane Sollee, Director of the Coalition for Marriage, Family and Couples Education, is also convinced of the importance of premarital programs. Research shows that a couple who spends at least twelve hours in a premarital education program decreases their chance of divorce five years out by fifty percent. But Sollee is quick to criticize programs that rely too heavily on premarital inventories. "An inventory looks to see if a couple agrees on all these different categories. If the couple agrees enough, then, oh, they can get married. You know, they talk about money, and having children, and sex, and religion, and politics. The problem is, this reinforces the idea that marriage is about compatibility. It's not. There's no such thing as a compatible couple. That's why the inventory model isn't used by most marriage educators."

The best marriage education programs focus on essential marriage skills, like communication and conflict resolution. Couples need to be told that they are going to disagree, that this is normal and expected, and will continue throughout a marriage. What is most important is that couples learn how to manage their disagreements. This is what good marriage education teaches.

Some marriage education courses are taught through church organizations, while others are housed within outpatient marriage and family clinics that provide such courses. There are also a few independent practitioners who provide programs for couples planning to marry.

For even more information on seeking out a course that best fits you, check out "Smart Marriages: The Coalition for Marriage, Family, and Couples Education" (http://www.smartmarriages.com/divorcepredictor.html). The website states that their "courses are not about what kind or type of marriage to build—they give couples the tools to build and maintain the marriage that fits their own dreams. These courses are taught in classroom settings—think teacher, flip chart, 'driver's ed for relationships.' This is not about therapy or encounter groups. Exposing private relationship issues and talking about your problems and feelings in front of others is not part of the process."

- Need more convincing to attend a class? "Marriage preparation courses are short, inexpensive, user-friendly, and empowering. Couples usually enjoy themselves as they gain mastery and become 'relationship smart.'"

The "Smart Marriages" website also provides succinct ideas about the benefits of premarital courses and explanations for the different kinds of programs that couples can choose:

- There are courses for different stages of a relationship and marriage. Couples can learn the skills at any stage—engaged, cohabiting, as newlyweds, as new parents, or after many years of marriage.

- The courses are also effective for couples facing serious distress or contemplating divorce. It turns out that when you learn to interact in new ways, the feelings of love CAN be revived—can come flowing back. You can learn to fall in love all over again.

- There are courses designed to teach high school and middle school students the skills for building good relationships and lasting marriages—to teach them what to look for in a mate.

- There are courses to help dating couples assess the strengths and weaknesses of their relationship and to learn how to improve the areas in which they have poor skills.

- There are courses designed specifically for the unique challenges of stepfamilies.

- And there are courses for couples facing the adventures of parenting—from first baby, to adolescents, to empty nests— or for dealing with sexual dysfunction, substance abuse, domestic violence, adultery, unemployment, dual careers, and illness.

- There are courses adapted for different denominations taught in churches, synagogues, and mosques.

- There are secular courses that are connected to no church or denomination which are taught in community centers, on military bases, in childbirth classes, in private practices, prisons, or at the county courthouse.

- The courses work equally well for any long-term committed relationship. Courses help cohabiting couples and can often give them the confidence to marry.

Conflict resolution was the main reason that Rajoot and his then-girlfriend Salandra sought out a marriage education course. They'd been dating for six years but were at an impasse over issues like finances and how often to visit Rajoot's family, who lived in another city.

"It was extremely helpful," Rajoot said. "It enabled us to talk through the issues we hadn't been able to talk about. Our communication skills really improved and deepened."

During the first of the required six sessions, both completed a relationship "inventory" to identify sources of conflict, then worked through problems under the guidance of the marriage educator.

To tackle their financial differences, Rajoot (the saver) and Salandra (the spender) were advised to document all their expenses and draw up a budget. Eating out was a major culprit, so they began cooking at home more.

"It gave us a foundation for our relationship," Rajoot said. "I'd recommend it for every couple."

Search out possible courses in your city or faith community that will fit your particular age and stage of your relationship. If you are considering or committed to marrying your partner, then let Google help you find a course in your city. It will pay great dividends.

Conclusion

Marriage is one of the toughest (and most rewarding) tests you'll ever face. Why not be prepared? A marriage preparation course or premarital counselling will give you and your spouse the tools you need to negotiate your relationship. Then it's practice, practice, practice!

Many people today think that attending marriage counselling or courses means you're admitting there are problems or issues in your relationship. Well, of course there are! No relationship is perfect. Premarital education exists to help you address important issues and prepare for the massive change that's about to happen in your lives. You're getting married! That might not sound like a big deal, but it is. Marriage is a shift in your relationship on every level. It's a psychological, emotional, and physical commitment to another person for the rest of your life. I'd say that warrants a class or two.

PART III

Don't Get Married . . . Unless You Can Commit to Fortifying Your Marriage

It is not a lack of love, but a lack of friendship that makes unhappy marriages.

—Friedrich Nietzsche

Introduction

If you have cleared the obstacles from your life and improved yourself so that you can bring your best self to a marriage—and you've found someone to embark on this journey with you—then this is a very exciting time for you! You are now ready for the greatest adventure of your life: giving your love away and learning how to receive love within a marriage. That might sound easy enough, to just be in love, right? Well, for some of us, the concept of loving openly and sharing our lives with another over the course of a marriage isn't so simple. But we can learn. There are specific skills that can assist you on how best to give and receive love.

Here's my guarantee: Any couple who has brought their best selves forward and truly commits to following my Three Pillars of a Fortified Marriage, will have a satisfying union. Of course, your marriage won't be without the usual challenges, disappointments, and disagreements that any couple encounters. For some, this will also include unexpected heartache, tragedy, and/or illness. However, these detours in your married life will NEVER be because of things or events that you have caused if you consistently follow my Three Pillars to Fortify Your Marriage.

Some of you might think that there are one or two rules you just can't follow. Then why proceed? Why would you want anything less than a satisfying marriage? Why do you want to mess with the most important decision of your life and mess with someone else's life? This ONE decision—whom you marry and who will marry you—will affect every other decision in your life, from the movies you attend, to where you live, to how healthy you will be. As the marriage goes, so goes your life. If you can't commit to following these simple rules, save yourself, and a possible spouse, the agony and expense of a failed marriage. PLEASE, I beg you, don't get married.

What if you're already married? What if you didn't do the hard work before you took your vows? Can you still have a satisfying marriage? The answer is a resounding yes! It IS possible, but all that preparation and work you avoided before will have to be caught up on. You and your spouse will need to make an even greater commitment and be open to tremendous individual and relationship growth.

It won't be easy. Many of you will be crushed and devastated in the trying. Some of you won't make it because there are too many obstacles and too many "don't get married characteristics" in your way. It might be unrealistic to have a satisfying marriage. That doesn't mean you shouldn't try, especially if you have children. For them, you will have to strive even harder, to prevent them from suffering the consequences of your marriage crumbling. Do all that you can and encourage your partner to do the same. Following these three simple pillars may just pull you both back from the brink.

For those of you who have prepared yourselves to be an excellent marriage candidate and for those of you who are already married and want to enhance and improve your marriage, read these next few chapters. Check off how many of the Three Pillars to Fortify Your Marriage you are prepared to commit to. If you are prepared to live by ALL of them, then your life and the life of your spouse will be joyous, trusting, and intimate—mentally, spiritually, emotionally, and physically. If you cannot live by these rules, or will not, or just aren't there yet, then do the right thing—don't get married!

Chapter 8

Three Pillars to Fortify Your Marriage

To a daughter contemplating the flaws in her marriage, a mother observes: *Remember, dear, it's being together at the end that really matters.*

—*Clare Booth Luce*, The Women, *Act 1, Scene 3*

Pillar #1: Regular Time Together as a Couple

In my clinical practice of seeing troubled couples, I make it a routine part of my assessment to ask: "How often are you dating or getting out together as a couple?" Invariably, those couples struggling in their marital relationships have stopped spending time together. Worse still, they have stopped dating.

It is one of the quickest assessment criteria I use to determine how far off the rails a particular couple has gone. When couples first become romantically involved, they want to spend all their time together. Over time, it's natural that this desire dissipates and the need to spend every possible minute together diminishes. Sometimes, spending time together is neglected because of the many demands of family life, work, children, leisure time, community service, and church involvement. This usually happens only for short periods of time, until life calms down. For couples in deep misery, the desire to be away from their spouse, to be separate from them as much as possible, doesn't dissipate. They find themselves simply not wanting to spend time together.

Couples in trouble have offered me innumerable excuses as to why they don't spend time together: "no money," "no babysitter," "no time," "no need to leave the home to spend time together," and "spending time as a couple takes away from family time." They'll say just about anything to avoid the issue. The real reason is that one or both spouses don't want to be together.

In all master marriages—marriages that have stood the test of time and been satisfying for both parties—spending regular time together is a given. Time is a recognized investment in the marriage that pays great dividends over the years.

I inquired of one couple, married thirty-five years with six children, "How did you decide to have regular time together? How did you do it with six kids?" Initially, they reported it was because the wife/ mother desperately needed a break from the home and childcare responsibilities.

"We had no money, so the early years were spent window shopping or window dreaming, a walk in the park, or an ice cream cone. Later, we progressed to dinner and a movie. And then we just settled into every Friday evening as 'date night.' We traded these date nights with friends. We cared for their children one night while on another they cared for ours. Occasionally our parents took a turn. The kids knew, our parents knew, and our friends knew that Friday nights were for us. There's something very different about being out in the world together, being seen as a couple, than there is sitting at home watching a movie together. Now, thirty-five years later, those Friday night dates have been one of the most satisfying aspects of our marriage. Some years we put a moratorium on discussing the children; other years, we set goals on those dates; and other times we just hung out. But knowing that we could look forward to one night a week with the most important person in our lives became sacred time for us."

This couple realized the importance of meaningful rituals in a marriage. Whether it's having a dinner conversation after work every night or taking a long walk, having something in place that allows you to stay in touch with each other's lives needs to be a foundational pillar for every marriage. Busy lives often interfere with being serendipitous and/or spontaneous as a couple; therefore, the ritualization of time spent together is often an effective way to make sure that it happens.

When I offer the assignment or advice for couples to have a regular "date night," they are often apprehensive if they have not spent time alone together for many weeks, months, or sometimes even years. I have found that assigning couples to carve out time for "dates" is not a cure for marital discord—especially if the time is spent staring blankly at each other or talking about a child's soccer game—but spending time together in troubled marriages is part of the repairing.

So, initially, I suggest to couples who have not been alone for some time, to start going to movies. This way, they don't have to talk. They can ease into becoming comfortable again in each other's presence and at least sit beside one another. And NO problem talk. You must leave your troubles at home. Dating is about connecting and getting to know each other, all over again. It might feel funny to make polite conversation with your spouse at first, but that's the place to start. Dating isn't about being parents or bill-payers or income-earners. It's about two people at a table or sitting in a theatre. Date nights should be about having fun and relaxing, NOT solving problems. Save all your issues for a "marriage meeting," a meeting where you do set aside time to discuss, resolve, and negotiate your marital problems.

Once couples become more comfortable together, I suggest they try to learn something together. Start engaging more openly, be willing to take risks in front of each other again (knowing that you're safe to succeed or fail), and create new memories. It's amazing how often learning and laughing go hand in hand.

When there has been significant repair and healing in the relationship, I then suggest, when possible, taking a vacation together without children, friends, or parents.

Never make excuses about being too busy or not having enough time to be together. Amazing couples make time for their spouses. It's about creating rituals. If one of your marital rituals is to make a regular "date night," then you don't have to wonder about when you'll go out or how long it's been. If you have dates on your calendar for the next three to four months, you are assured that you will take time to play together, have fun together, and carry on a conversation on a regular basis without interruption.

Scheduling getaways is another important decision every married couple should make. Once or twice a year, set aside time for a twenty-four to forty-eight hour getaway for just the two of you. Or, better still, one week once a year is even more desirable. Can Grandma, sister, Auntie, or good friends watch the kids? Can you trade childcare with another couple? With a date on the calendar, the details are ready to be determined and the plans are put in place. This time away is essential for couples to remember what it's like to sleep until noon together or to spend the day hiking trails. This is when you take the time to do things like languishing in bed, have grownup time, or even long dinners like you did when you were dating. It's the time when you can talk while not making lunches for children, driving to swimming lessons, or pacing through rush hour.

Keep courtship alive in your marriage. Date once a week! Week in, week out, month in, month out, year in, year out. Go out into the world as a couple. Go for a walk, to dinner, to shop, to hike, anywhere, as long as you are by yourselves. Enjoy each other's company and make memories together. Dating your spouse will pay great dividends in your marriage.

Ancient Scripture tells us, "This is now bone of my bone and flesh of my flesh—therefore shall a man leave his father and his mother, and shall cleave unto his wife and they shall be one flesh." You can't become "one flesh" or one in heart and purpose unless you spend regular, committed time together. You can't become one flesh if you are continuously doing things apart from one another.

Pillar #2: Regular praise and affection

The greatest weakness of most humans is their hesitancy to tell others how much they love them while they're still alive.

—Orlando Battista

Then there was the guy who loved his wife so much, he almost told her.

—Unknown

Start spreading the news. Don't let the sun go down without complimenting each other. Everyone loves to hear good news. Look for the strengths and qualities that you love about your spouse, pay attention to his or her random acts of kindness towards you or others, and notice when your spouse is extending themselves.

Express your appreciation for any and all things you admire and love about your partner.

In his book *Why Marriages Succeed or Fail* (1994), John Gottman claims there is a magic 5-1 ratio (five positives to one negative) that can predict divorce or stability with high accuracy. Positive stuff includes showing interest, asking questions, being kind, giving a hug, or being empathetic. Negative stuff includes criticism, hostility, or hurting your spouse's feelings. Successful couples say or do at least five positive things for each negative interaction with their partner. Not an easy feat. Gottman's wise advice, based on the research, is to accentuate the positive and minimize (though you won't eliminate) the negative.

If you do something negative to hurt your partner's feelings, then you have to do five positive things to offset a critical or adverse interaction. Negativity, in any form, has a greater ability to inflict pain and damage. We carry it with us longer and bear the scars more deeply.

Positive interactions, on the other hand, build up what Gottman calls "the reservoir of positive feeling." Like a savings account into which you make regular deposits to be withdrawn on a rainy day. Couples who have reservoirs of positive feelings use some of this when they are criticized to offset their hurt feelings so that things balance out.

How would you rate the ratio of positive and negative interactions in your relationship? Do you have at least a 5 to 1? There should be five hugs, compliments, or squeezes of the arm for every roll of the eyes, critical comment, or blaming.

Respect, gratitude, affection, friendship, and noticing what's going right are "habits of mind" which create a culture of appreciation. Show your gratitude for your spouse every day.

The Time is Now
If you are ever going to love me,
Love me now, while I can know
The sweet and tender feelings
Which from true affection flow.
Love me now
While I am living.
Do not wait until I'm gone
And then have it chiselled in marble,

Sweet words on ice-cold stone.
If you have tender thoughts of me,
Please tell me now.
Unknown

Pillar #3: Regular intimacy

Passion is the quickest to develop, and the quickest to fade. Intimacy develops more slowly, and commitment more gradually still.

—Robert Sternberg

Scheduling intimacy is another ritual married couples should adopt, especially couples with kids. Too often we expect physical intimacy to always be spontaneous, but in a life with children and work, the pace is frantic and the exhaustion is constant. Spontaneity happens occasionally, but not often enough for a healthy love life. Smart couples who make a commitment to a regular schedule of intimacy find this ritual one of the best decisions they've made for their marriage. For the person with a higher desire for intimacy, it assures them sex will happen. For the partner with a lesser desire for intimacy, it builds anticipation and helps them prepare mentally and physically for the time together. More sex means better sex.

"Just do it," says divorce-busting therapist Michele Weiner-Davis, author of *The Sex-Starved Marriage* (2003). That's not exactly conventional wisdom for married couples with an unsatisfying sex life. Marriage therapists usually like to talk about feelings, relationship issues, and communication skills before we concentrate on physical intimacy.

But Weiner-Davis thinks mismatched sexual desire is not merely a symptom of a troubled relationship, but a problem of not enough physical intimacy. She suggests that, sometimes, it's better to get couples to address their physical needs first. In other words, when a lack of intimacy is the problem in a marriage, couples should have sex, even if one or the other (or both) isn't in the mood.

The late Shirley Glass, author of *Not "Just Friends,"* which explores marital infidelity, doesn't want readers to view Michele Weiner-

Davis's work as going back to the days when women had a "wifely duty." Even in this post-feminist period, women still have the option of saying no.

Having regular and enjoyable sex usually isn't a problem for couples in the first year of marriage, when passions are still running high. But the flames of desire tend to dwindle over time, and for a variety of reasons. First, of course, are physical changes—aging, childbirth, changes in hormone levels, or medications like antidepressants or birth control pills that can diminish desire. So, too, can other factors like fatigue or stress.

It can get complicated. A spouse who wants to have sex more often may feel angry, betrayed, or rejected when he or she is refused. The partner with less interest may feel pressured or annoyed by the other person's frequent advances. The result is an escalation in the problem, a vicious circle of repeated injuries and misunderstanding. Couples will argue over seemingly unrelated matters, becoming short-tempered and insensitive to their partners, and much more open to infidelities.

A mismatched level of sexual desire isn't the issue. Ultimately, the issue is whether a couple is willing or unwilling to address that problem. Weiner-Davis claims that the recent work of Dr. Rosemary Basson, a Canadian researcher and expert in human sexuality, reinforces her point of view. Dr. Basson found that the urge to become sexual in women often follows, rather than precedes, feeling aroused.

Agree to be affectionate. Still, this message could be misinterpreted. It isn't suggesting that a wife submit to her husband whenever he has the desire for a sexual connection, but it also doesn't mean that the decision to have sex should be entirely in the hands of the person with the lowest sex drive. Some women believe there's something wrong with having sex simply because your partner wants it, and that's a problem.

Sometimes, women are reluctant to begin any kind of sexual intimacy because their partner will take it as a commitment to go all the way. Couples need to agree to be affectionate, to snuggle, touch, and fondle. Sometimes this will lead to a full sexual experience and sometimes it won't. There is no ideal amount of sex in a marriage. There's only too little when one or both partners are dissatisfied with its frequency.

Claude and Chantal came to my clinical practice after being married just two years. Claude was anxious to tell me that the main conflict in their marriage was the infrequency of their lovemaking. Chantal looked down, seemingly shamed. When I explored further, this was Claude's main complaint, not Chantal's. Claude persisted with his complaints about Chantal and, in total frustration, said, "We don't even kiss anymore."

Chantal replied in a snippy tone, "Because as soon as we kiss, it always leads to intercourse."

"And what would be wrong with that?" I asked.

She looked astonished. "Well, we have a child, meals to fix, laundry to do, and you can be sure HE doesn't do a thing in any of those areas."

Another one of the most common complaints of North American couples. Husbands want more sex; wives want more help with household chores and childcare. Here's the deal, which research substantiates: husbands will help more with household chores if their wives will have more sex; wives will have more sex if husbands will help more with household chores. I offered an idea to the couple of ritualizing household chores and sex: Claude helps three evenings a week with dishes, bathing, and putting their one-year-old to bed, and Chantal reserves a minimum of one night a week for lovemaking.

Surprisingly, it was the husband who questioned this assignment. "But what if I've had a rough day and am really tired or not in the mood for kitchen detail or bathing our son or I have to work again after dinner?" It was astounding how this very capable accountant could handle international finance issues by day, but the thought of doing dishes and/or bathing his son could completely exhaust him in the evening. Of course, he would never be too tired to refuse sex if offered! I didn't want to offend him, so instead I said, "Yes, there are a lot of demands with a young family and your work. But would you be willing to experiment with this schedule for even three weeks to see what effect it might have on you both being more satisfied in your relationship?"

He agreed that he would be willing to experiment. I turned to Chantal, who had been listening intently.

"And why would I be in the mood to make love with someone with that attitude about being a husband and father in the evenings?"

"What difference do you think it would make on your evening happiness scale if Claude would pitch in three nights a week?"

"Well, it would certainly be better than nothing, but he should help every night."

"Yes," I said, "that would be ideal, and making love once a week with a reluctant wife is also not ideal, but better than nothing. Would you be willing to experiment with weekly sex, even if you're not in the mood?"

She agreed. When they returned some three weeks later, the tension between the two had dramatically decreased. They were actually joking with one another. The husband said, "Things are great. We've made love once a week and one week twice."

There was no mention about him helping with dishes or bathing their son. "Well, that's great, yet I'm equally curious about the other part of the experiment."

"Oh, you mean the household and bathing stuff? That was easy. No problem. Actually, I even made dinner one night."

"Wow!" I teased. "You really are going overboard. And what has been your wife's reaction?"

"Well, she's sure been a lot more pleasant when I come home, especially on the nights I've committed to helping more. And I think she even enjoyed the sex. . . . Well, did you?"

Chantal said that she was surprised that even if she wasn't in the mood for sex that once they began, her desire and enjoyment increased. "I could not believe the difference in my mood on the evenings when Claude helped me. And I found I enjoyed making love more if it was on one of those evenings."

Ritualizing intimacy to this extent is sometimes necessary when there have been huge gaps in intimacy over a prolonged time. I've found in my practice that often a quid pro quo for increased intimacy works well in these situations.

SIDEBAR

Five Steps Toward Better Married Sex

1. Don't stick your head in the sand. If you aren't happy with your sex life, seek help. Read a book, talk to a doctor.

2. If you are the more highly-sexed spouse, talk to your partner about the "f-word"—feelings. Don't shut down and go into a cave or get angry and resentful. Anger and isolation aren't very good aphrodisiacs.

3. Tune into your spouse's turn-ons. Men may like videos and lingerie, but their wives may be into something else entirely—like a little help around the house. Maybe what she really needs is a chance to sleep in or for someone else to fold the laundry.

4. If you are the less sexual person, consider having sex more often. You'll feel more sexual pleasure and you'll get the spouse of your dreams in return.

5. Find the right resource to boost your sexuality if desire is still a problem. There are sex therapists and treatments that can be effective.

(From Michele Weiner-Davis, author of The Sex-Starved Marriage/A Couple's Guide to Boosting Their Marriage Libido [Simon & Schuster 2003].)

Conclusion

The Three Pillars to Fortify Your Marriage

Pillar #1: Regular time together as a couple

Pillar #2: Regular praise and affection

Pillar #3: Regular intimacy

Can it really be this simple? In short, yes! These three pillars are THE most important to fortify your marriage! If you and your partner can commit to all three, your chances of a long and happy union are excellent. Nurture your relationship by staying connected, compassionate, and intimate. Regulate these factors, so you both know what to expect. It's so much easier to face the world when you know you have a spouse who looks forward to spending time with you, tells you you're loved, and even helps with the dishes knowing sex is just hours away!

By taking the guesswork out of the affection

in your marriage, you fortify yourselves against the many temptations waiting outside your door.

Chapter 9

Eight Hot Tips to Sustain Your Fortified Marriage

My wife tells me that if I ever decide to leave, she is coming with me.

—Jon Bon Jovi

1. Never talk about or threaten separation or divorce.

If you made wedding vows to be there for one another in sickness and health, in good times and bad, for richer or poorer, and you really want to stay married, then never talk about or threaten separation or divorce. Don't put that idea into your head or into your spouse's. It never serves you well to threaten unless you are prepared to follow through. Deal breakers for marriage are affairs, addictions, and abuse (emotional, mental, and physical). But these deal breakers should be clear before you marry. Anything else requires mature adults to learn how to resolve conflict or navigate around it.

2. The Forty-Eight Hour Principle: No Dumping Allowed.

When conflict, disappointment, or hurt arises (and it will), talk about it within forty-eight hours. After two days of sitting on an issue, there is simply no point in bringing it up, other than to inflict pain on your partner or instigate a new fight. Instead, avoid storing old hurts and resentments in a garbage can and then dumping them on your spouse days, weeks, or months later. The more time that passes, the more the hurts and slights can become exaggerated, and then it's difficult to remember the marital incidents that inflicted the pain in the first place. Commit to discussing hurts and disappointments within forty-eight hours or not at all.

Ancient scripture says, "Come and let us reason together!" Reasoning together is at its best when it happens in a context of love within forty-eight hours.

In my clinical practice, I have offered this

idea to numerous couples to break the cycle of saving up grievances and then dumping them once they have a wheelbarrow full. When dumped in this manner, it's frequently done with exaggerated intensity and anger. Suddenly, that little comment he made last week or last year is a point of burning rage. In full drama-queen style, time and proximity have magnified it to a giant pile of angst with unreasonable proportions. Rather than looking at that one incident, you find yourself looking at all the neglected resentments combined. That comment, plus the forgotten birthday, plus all the evenings on the couch while you've put the kids to bed, plus that time at the shopping mall, plus that comment at last year's Thanksgiving dinner at your parents . . . it all becomes overwhelming.

Sharing within forty-eight hours or not at all helps to prioritize which issues are worth raising and which are not. When something happens that hurts you or upsets you, ask yourself if it's worth bringing it to your spouse's attention right away or within forty-eight hours. If it is, then have the discussion. If it isn't, then you have to question whether it's worth holding on to. If an issue isn't important enough to bring up within forty-eight hours—and let's face it, many probably aren't—then you have to let it go.

After implementing this advice, one husband told me that he was more willing to listen to his wife, knowing he wouldn't "receive an atomic bomb of complaints" that she had been saving up for months. Their marriage improved dramatically and his wife confirmed that her husband was much more attentive when she shared hurts within forty-eight hours, rather than exploding with a laundry list of his slights and sarcastic comments two months later. For her, her shoulders became lighter as she realized that she didn't need to constantly carry around ammunition to use against her husband. She could simply decide to either discuss it or let it go.

3. Learn to be spiritually grounded and centred in your life.

Everyone needs to feel grounded, centred and, at the same time, moving forward in one's personal life. This usually occurs in the spiritual domain where we all are seeking meaning, purpose, and connection in our lives. To enable this to happen, each of us needs to learn how to tap into our own spiritual sources for personal, inner renewal. By learning what works for each of us, we can bring a peaceful and evolving self to our primary relationship.

Commit to learning about yourself, expanding your point of view, and extending yourself to the world for a purpose and meaning beyond yourself. For some, the primary meaning, purpose and significant connections in their lives will be devotion to and spending time with family, friends, and their life's career. Others expand to volunteering in their community, perhaps with the elderly, homeless, or serving on boards. Others will engage in spiritual practices such as walking meditation, praying, reading books on forgiveness or compassion, and/or taking courses that invite reflection about spirituality in their lives. Still others expand their spirituality within a faith or religious community and attend and serve in a church, synagogue, mosque, or temple.

Many young persons and senior couples widen their meaning, purpose, and connection in their lives through service to others by volunteering internationally to work in orphanages, AIDS hospices, and/or help to construct pure water systems. Learning and serving gives your life meaning, purpose, and connection. You then live your life congruent with those beliefs. Sharing your ways of inner renewal together can increase your marital solidarity.

At times, it may be necessary to look outward to explore individual issues or obstacles when meaning and purpose in your life are being questioned, troubling you, or causing angst.

In some situations, it may be enough to disclose troubles to your spouse, a trusted friend, or family member. In other situations, a few counselling sessions may be helpful. Sometimes changing the context, like a needed vacation, can help to gain new insights into personal issues that may arise.

Spiritual or religious practices can assist in keeping couples together. Studies show that people who marry within a religious community are somewhat more likely to stay married than people with no affiliation. Marrying someone of the same or similar religion also improves the odds of staying together, even if one partner converts.

As individuals and couples age, more reflection naturally occurs about what is important, meaningful, purposeful, and worthy of their time and attention. The more a couple evolves similarly in their beliefs about the purpose and meaning of their lives, the more satisfaction in the marriage.

4. Put your marriage first, children second.

The trend in our society is for families to be more child-focused than in the past two generations. Often, couples elevate raising children to a single-minded goal of the marriage. Having a family is of course incredibly worthy, enjoyable (mostly), and satisfying. It also requires great devotion, caring, and responsibility for parents. But adults who see raising children as their only mission end up burdening their children. It is not a child's job to make adults feel worthwhile, needed, and loved. Distinctions need to be made between being parents and being spouses.

In order to be good parents, you first have to be good spouses. In a supportive, committed relationship, children can be raised in a loving, stable environment. When there is an imbalance within your core relationship, the whole family suffers. Suddenly, parents aren't partners and sides are taken. An equal and fulfilling union stands the best possible chance of raising happy children.

5. Seek common interests.

Develop a common interest that you can share together. You're going to be spending a life together. It's nice to have an activity to share that helps you enjoy that time together. Whether it's movies, a favourite computer game, cycling, or garage sales, find your common interests and turn them into pleasurable experiences. Some couples share all their activities; some only share one. The most important aspect is that you have regular time together. Over the years, these activities and interests may change and vary according to age, health, and child rearing.

6. Share your lives through emotional intimacy.

Create and share a private world where you confide deeply about life, joys, fears, hurts, frustrations, and challenges. Talk often and openly about feelings and wonderment. Stay in touch with the details of each other's emotional lives. Use each other as sounding boards for talking through a problem out loud, working through issues, and gaining a valued perspective. Turn to each other for advice and comfort. Be a good listener. Show empathy and concern.

SIDEBAR

Surprise!

Make your marriage full of special surprises. Marriages are more alive and exciting when surprises are sprinkled into them. Surprise your spouse with a vacation, a special date night, flowers, an iPhone, or anything else that excites them.

---

7. Operate as a team, except perhaps in housework.

Coordinate schedules and activities together. Plan and make decisions together. Support both your own family commitments and the extended family obligations as a team. Parent as a team. Manage money as a team. Even when illness strikes, couples who manage the illness from a "we are going to fight this together" perspective cope much better than those where it's "your" illness rather than "our" illness. Being a team does not necessarily mean having equal responsibilities in each area, but recognizing each other's strengths and competencies and agreeing *as a team* who will take the lead.

For example, in the area of money management, one of you may be great at developing a savings plan online with an Excel spreadsheet; while in the area of planning activities, the other spouse may be the more competent at scheduling monthly calendars for couple and family activities.

Share household responsibilities as equals. In theory, this sounds easy, but in reality this is one area where I have encouraged exceptions to the operating as a team rule. What is it about vacuuming, cleaning toilets, and washing windows that can invite such angst in couples? Some love cleaning; some do not. There are just so many differences between men and women about what it means to participate equally in household responsibilities. These disparities are based on previous experiences in their families-of-origin, cultural differences, and the dramatic changes in women's roles both in and out of the home, especially in the past forty years. These many differences result in too many couples keeping score about who cleans what, who cleans the best, and how often. For some dual-income couples, there is just too much duelling over housework.

Anne Marie was a clean freak while her husband, Jason, had no interest in housework. He had been the only boy in a household of three older sisters; therefore, he escaped housework and had no desire in increasing his housecleaning skills as a hard-working husband and father. His wife, however, wouldn't accept this attitude and was continuously nagging him (repetitive encouragement, as women prefer to think of it) to participate in housework. When I asked what he thought about his contributions to the home, he said, "I think I do my share, but it's never enough for her. So I've been begging her to get a cleaning lady."

Anne Marie rebuffed this suggestion. "You know we can't afford that!"

Stephanie Coontz, a marriage historian, adds some insight into understanding the differences between men and women and household chores. In her book *A Strange Stirring: The Feminine Mystique and American Women at the Dawn of the 1960s* (2012), she offers that women consistently underestimate their husbands' contributions. They don't apply the same value to them as they do to their own efforts. However, studies have shown that women still spend about twenty-eight hours each week on housework, while their husbands log about sixteen hours. There are also great disparities in the perceptions of childcare, and even greater still when considering cooking and housecleaning. More than fifty percent of men claim most or half of the work, while seventy percent of women report doing it all.

With some couples, I have suggested changing

roles for a day or a week. For example, the husband/father does all the grocery shopping and cleans out their daughters' thermoses and lunch boxes. She plays board games with their daughters and hoses out their wading pool. Changing roles is an attempt to have couples free themselves of traditional divisions of labour.

For a variety of reasons, negotiating around shared housework for busy working couples, and especially those with children, rarely gets solved to the satisfaction of either husband or wife, even when there are attempts to equally share the household cleaning. So, perhaps somewhat surprisingly, Jason's suggestion is a good one. For double-income couples to resolve the conflict over housecleaning, the most successful intervention is to hire a cleaning lady, or man. (Where I live, there is a wonderful cleaning service called "Man Maid," and yes, it's a man who comes to clean. Wouldn't we all like to be married to him?)

When I further explored Anne Marie's belief that they couldn't afford a cleaning lady, it became apparent that this was a constraining belief based on her own family-of-origin. Anne Marie's parents could never afford a cleaning lady, and she would be embarrassed to tell her parents that they employed one. I learned that she was from a family of five children, with a traditional stay-at-home mom and a single-income dad. Jason replied, "But we're both working full time, two kids, and church responsibilities. Our lives are very different from your family."

I prodded Jason to be a bit more compassionate about Anne Marie's feeling of embarrassment. "Do you hear that Anne Marie is more concerned about money or embarrassment with her parents?"

Suddenly, Jason got it. "Well, I never knew before that you would be embarrassed. I can understand that. Unfortunately, your father wasn't the best at making a living for the family. He was always jumping from one job to another. But I would like you not to be so stressed out over how our home looks, so you can enjoy the kids more, and me."

"I'm glad I could finally say it out loud about being embarrassed. I guess I've also been embarrassed about being embarrassed. But seriously, where would we get the money?"

"Well, we have other expenses I'd be willing to

cut back, like giving up attending one hockey game a month if you would be willing to not have a monthly massage," Jason said.

"REALLY? You would give up a hockey game? Okay, you have a deal. But my friends tell me that they have trouble finding a cleaning person that cleans like they do. Well, I guess that's something I just have to let go."

About two months later, this couple returned and reported that the intervention of having a cleaning woman, twice a month, was working wonderfully for them. When I asked who has appreciated it the most, Anne Marie answered, "Definitely me. Jason wasn't unhappy with the house before. He was just unhappy with me nagging him all the time."

This wasn't the major issue that this couple consulted about, but it was one that kept coming up while we were trying to focus on the major one. Once the housecleaning issue was put to rest, they both had renewed energy for improving their relationship skills.

I once encountered a rather extreme solution to conflict about household chores.

I met with a couple who were both high-income earners as physicians with very busy practices and three school-age boys. When I suggested they retain some outside cleaning assistance, the wife was the most receptive to the idea. The husband said he would prefer spending their money on other things, but at the same time was not willing to increase his contributions to household responsibilities.

When they returned to our next session, I was stunned to learn that they had engaged a woman, not to just come monthly or weekly, but to come *daily* (to make the beds, tidy, clean, and some prep for dinners). I asked how they had come to this solution and the wife replied, "I asked myself, 'What would Angelina Jolie and Brad Pitt do?' I knew they have live-in help, so I thought I would do the next best thing."

I asked the husband, "And how's this working for you?"

"We should have done this three or four years ago. I've got my good-natured wife back."

For some dual-income couples, the differences in perception about the amount of housework that each does and all the angst around it *can* be solved. Employing someone to clean has the dual benefit of increasing marital satisfaction and increasing the cleanliness of the home.

8. Never place yourself in a situation where you would be tempted to have an affair.

Bad marriages don't cause infidelity; infidelity causes bad marriages.

—Frank Pittman

Honour your vows of fidelity. Infidelity wreaks havoc in marriages. And infidelity is *preventable*. In the ups and downs of life, the only thing you have to fall back on is your character and honour in keeping the promises you make. That's true in life in general and in your marriage. There is only one person in your life you have vowed to honour and be loyal to—your spouse.

Over the past few years, infidelity (emotional and sexual) has become the most common marital issue I've encountered in my clinical practice.

Avoiding the temptation of affairs will save such unnecessary hurt and misery from which there is often no possibility for healing. The betrayal and distrust that follow an affair are usually too tremendous to overcome.

My best advice for avoiding affairs? Have strong boundaries and don't allow emotional intimacy within friendships. Flirting a little with your "work husband" might seem harmless on the surface, but it holds the potential to destroy your marriage. Most affairs occur at the workplace, so it is doubly important to set rules and boundaries for how you will function at work.

Do you have lunch at work with the same colleague alone each day? Do you complain about your spouse to someone of the opposite sex at the gym and they seem to understand so well? Are you enjoying working overtime with a co-worker of the opposite sex more than you enjoy the anticipation of going home to your spouse? These are all warning signs that you are tempting yourself beyond what is reasonable.

Intimacies outside your core relationship take energy and closeness away from your spouse. Those creative juices you burn crafting cute little jokes for someone else could be spent on the man or woman you share your life with.

Beyond taking momentum away from your marriage, these dalliances can quickly grow into more than you consciously intended. Often, when our spouses are busy and life isn't leaving time for the little intrigues we used to get while dating, we turn to outside sources to get the thrills we miss. A whispered word here, a shared secret there, can lead to the blossoming of emotional connections and ultimately to the betrayal of your vows. Instead, focus on the one you married and put your energy into spicing up that relationship.

One way to think of the appropriate boundaries is through the useful metaphor of walls and windows as suggested by the late Dr. Shirley Glass in her classic book *Not "Just Friends"* (2003). Keep the windows open at home; put up privacy walls with others who would threaten your marriage. ONLY associate with friends and family members who are "friends" of your marriage! True friends won't criticize or denigrate your spouse. They won't judge or manipulate your relationship. True friends WANT your marriage to succeed!

SIDEBAR

Five practical rules to prevent emotional or physical intimacy with anyone other than your spouse:

1. Whether your spouse is with you or not, behave as though they are. Don't do anything that you wouldn't do with your husband or wife standing beside you.

2. Don't spend personal time with someone you could be attracted to, especially if they are single.

3. Don't talk about problems in your marriage with anyone who could be a threat to it.

4. Avoid the very appearance or the slightest temptation that can arise when men and women spend time alone together who are NOT married to one another.

5. Don't troll the Internet for trouble!

An online affair is a lot easier than sneaking out of the house in the middle of the night. The Internet may soon become the most common form of emotional infidelity. Most spouses feel as betrayed, angry, and hurt by online infidelity as they would if skin-to-skin adultery had taken place. Couples in my practice report that what started as innocent, friendly exchanges online progressed quickly to strong desires for sexual relationships. The use and role of the Internet needs to be as much a part of marital openness as joint bank accounts.

SIDEBAR

Couple Rules for Internet use:

- Share your password with your spouse.

- Make it clear to your spouse that he or she is welcome to look through your computer emails.

- Make sure your spouse knows or is aware of everyone in your "buddy/friend" lists or knows that she has access to the list at any time.

- Do not search for prior boyfriends/girlfriends online.

- Social Networking sites like Facebook/Twitter/LinkedIn are the exceptions. Former partners may contact you regardless of whether you initiate contact. In these situations, it is always best to inform your partner and ask for their input/recommendation. This two-way communication and decision-making process builds trust. Make sure to set your relationship status to "Married" to alert others to the fact that you are taken and post a picture of yourself and your spouse.

Conclusion

Words have power to hurt or heal. Whether they're shouted in anger—"I swear I'll divorce you!"—or dumped on your spouse daily, they all have power to hurt. It's up to you to control them. How can you make sure your marriage stands the test of time? Be mindful of your words and actions. Don't put yourself at risk of having an affair by trolling the Internet, looking for trouble, or spending an undue amount of time with someone of the opposite sex other than your spouse. In the movie "When Harry Met Sally," one of the characters asked if men and women can just be friends. I believe men and women can be friends as long as they are not alone together for regular or prolonged periods of time. Increased interaction increases intimacy. Harry believed that men and women cannot be friends as men always desire to have sex with someone they find attractive. Honour the commitment you've made to your spouse. Have the courage of your convictions!

Be a team, you and your love, by putting your

marriage first, above all else. Yours is a sacred bond, so keep it that way!

Chapter 10

Love Holds It All Together

I like not only to be loved, but to be told that I am loved; the realm of silence is large enough beyond the grave.

—George Eliot

Love is not something people feel, but something people try to express no matter how they feel.

—Frank Pittman

Love, love, love your spouse.

Marriage IS a most wonderful and incredible union. It is an outstanding and magnificent relationship. Nowhere is there the possibility for more comfort, more joy, more security, or more love.

Marriage is also sacred. If one does not believe marriage is sacred, it is easier to walk away when problems arise, easier to deceive in order to fulfill one's own selfish needs and passions, and easier to abuse another because you believe you have the right.

When spouses view a marriage union as sacred, they make an agreement to evolve within that relationship together. This puts them on equal footing. When two people are committed to finding solutions to problems together, they work as a team. The solutions in any marriage have to work for both participants, or they won't work at all. Knowing you can rely on your spouse to stay and face the realities of life allows you to truly be yourself. Of course you'll stumble at times and fall at others, but you'll always know your partner will see you through because your union is sacred. That knowledge brings more than superficial comfort; it confirms within your deepest soul that you are not alone in your marriage.

Love your spouse above all others.

To reinforce this commitment to one another, make your marriage a higher priority than any other relationship in your life, including friends, family, or children. No one in this world can be as important as your husband or wife. Without them, all those other relationships change and shift. When marriage is the nucleus of your family, the rest of your connections are stronger.

Show love through actions on a daily basis. Anticipate and meet your spouse's emotional needs through daily acts of love and consideration. It's easy in today's fast-paced world to get caught up in our own day and drama. Take a minute to step back and ask what your spouse might need, then follow through. A simple "I love you" can go a long way. So can cleaning up the kitchen once in a while!

Be there for each other in times of joy and times of sorrow.

We've all heard the vow—in good times and in bad—and it's there for a reason. In times of joy, we create happy memories, warm connections, and fond celebration. Those are the moments we all live for. In a marriage, they sustain us through the day-to-day and through the bad times. In times of crisis, tragedy, or darkness, married couples form bonds of strength and commitment. They see within their partner's support, the depth of their connection and the importance of being there for one another.

Give Your Support Freely.

Do not think of it as a sacrifice to encourage and support your spouse's goals, growth, dreams, and wishes. This is married life. Have a willing heart about pleasing your partner and responding to requests and concerns. This is love, freely given even when it is difficult or inconvenient. It might sound clichéd, but when you give love, you receive love. This is especially true in a healthy marriage. The more supported your spouse feels, the more they will reciprocate. It becomes a cycle of caring, loving gestures that add up to a happy life. Give, and then give a little more. Instead of trying to get your way, try to give a little, then give a little more. In other words, practice thinking "We" instead of "Me."

In marriage, there is an expectation of each doing their fair share when it comes to housework, childcare, and fidelity. Generosity with your love means going above and beyond the ordinary expectations with small acts of service and making an extra effort to be affectionate.

When a spirit of generosity exists, it leads to both spouses on average being happier in the marriage. And being happier invites feeling more loved, and feeling more loved invites feeling happier! A lovely virtuous cycle for which to strive.

The song "It's You I Like" by the late and wonderful Mr. Fred Rogers has always touched me. He knew what it meant to love another, to love someone for who they are deep down inside, and he expressed it so simply and beautifully.

"It's You I Like"

It's you I like,
It's not the things you wear.
It's not the way you do your hair,
But it's you I like.
The way you are right now
The way down deep inside you
Not the things that hide you
Not your diplomas . . .
They're just beside you.
But it's you I like,
Every part of you,
Your skin, your eyes, your feelings,
Whether old or new.
I hope that you'll remember
Even when you're feeling blue,
That it's you I like,
It's you yourself, it's you,
It's you I like!

© Fred M. Rogers, Used with permission

Conclusion

Every once in a while, look at your spouse and remind yourself that this is the person you *chose* to share your life with. This is the man or woman you have vowed to love and cherish—and who promised you the same. Love them. You've committed yourself to each other and, if you've been following the advice in this book, to fortifying that union against all the elements and pressures of the modern world. Love each other within your marriage, always open to changing and evolving together. Love, maturity, and strength of character—that's always been the secret to a fulfilling and mutually satisfying relationship and essential in the wonderful world of marriage.

Final Thoughts

Marry or Not?

"Any fool can have a trophy wife, but it takes a real man to have a trophy marriage."

—Diane Sollee

So that's it! If you are single, can you now more honestly answer the questions: "Am I a good candidate for marriage? Is my partner?" I hope you can answer these more confidently now that you know some of the most important red flags to observe when in a relationship. Now you can also reflect on your own personal characteristics and issues that need improving and/or working through, to ensure you're bringing your best self forward in your relationship. You also know the essential communication and relationship skills to be learned and what deficit experiences to avoid. Now it's all up to you to decide if you should marry or not at this time, or maybe never.

If you are already cohabiting or married, then it's all up to the two of you! Are the three pillars to fortify your marriage solidly in place (regular time together, regular praise and affection, and regular intimacy)? What are the relationship and communication skills that need to be improved? Are you together in your beliefs about the meaning and purpose of your lives and marriage? There will, of course, be times in any relationship when one person is more interested in having an individual or couple growth spurt than the other; when one is more concerned with issues in the marriage than the other. But all the while, your marriage should always be moving forward in ways that are satisfying to you both.

Most importantly, are you able to give your love away, to be generous with your love, and to prioritize your spouse above all other relationships?

There is nothing magic about the recommendations offered in this book, but an ongoing miracle happens when they are regularly practiced. Yes, PRACTICE! Malcolm Gladwell, the renowned social commentator, recommends in his book *Outliers: The Story of Success* (2008), that to be an expert and/or competent requires 10,000 hours of persistent practice. Are you willing to put in the time? Ten thousand hours of persistent practice of the skills required for a magnificent marriage? If not, PLEASE do not marry. It's okay if you decide to not marry now, or maybe never. You can still use your time wisely to learn about yourself and how to give your best to the world. If you do decide to marry, you will be ahead of the game—having already done the necessary work on yourself and being able to recognize your equal in a mate.

For those of you already married, I hope this book will give you renewed hope and appreciation of how to have a magnificent and awesome marriage. I have offered the most essential skills and behaviours that, if implemented, are guaranteed to improve and sustain your marriage in its enjoyment, satisfaction, and longevity. There will be slip-ups, setbacks, and shortcuts that go nowhere, but get back on track fast and continue on your marvellous journey. You CAN do it! You as a couple CAN do it!

I wish you well in whatever you decide is best for your life at this time: to marry or not, to stay married or divorce. Who knows, I may yet try it myself some day. In the meantime, I wish to leave you with some convincing and compelling reasons for why marriage matters. Because it does matter; in fact, research shows that marriage, good marriages, might just save the world.

(Reprinted with permission from The Institute for American Values. [2005]. *Why Marriage Matters: Thirty Conclusions from the Social Sciences* [2nd ed.]. Retrieved from http://americanvalues.org/pdfs/why_marriage_matters2.pdf.)

Why Marriage Matters

Family

1. Marriage increases the likelihood that fathers and mothers have good relationships with their children.

2. Cohabitation is not the same as marriage. Cohabiting couples on average are less committed, less faithful, and more likely to

break up than married couples.

3.　Growing up outside an intact marriage increases the likelihood that children will themselves divorce or become unwed parents.

4.　In almost every known human society, marriage exists as a way of regulating the reproduction of children, families, and society.

5.　Marriage typically fosters better romantic and parental relationships compared to other family forms, such as cohabitation. Individuals who have a firm commitment to marriage as an ideal are more likely to invest themselves in their marriage and to enjoy happier marriages.

6. Marriage has important biological consequences for adults and children. For instance, marriage appears to reduce men's testosterone levels, and girls who grow up in an intact, married family appear to have a relatively later onset of puberty.

Economics

7.　Divorce and unmarried childbearing increase poverty for both children and mothers.

8. Married couples seem to build more wealth on average than singles or cohabiting couples.

9. Marriage reduces poverty and material hardship (for example, missing a meal or failing to pay rent) for disadvantaged women and their children.

10. African Americans and Latinos benefit economically from marriage.

11. Married men earn more money than do single men with similar education and job histories.

12. Parental divorce (or failure to marry) appears to increase children's risk of dropping out of high school.

13. Parental divorce reduces the likelihood that children will graduate from college and achieve high-status jobs.

Physical Health and Longevity

14. Children who live with their own two married parents enjoy better physical health

than do children in other family forms.

15. Parental marriage is associated with a sharply lower risk of infant mortality.

16. Marriage is associated with reduced rates of drug and alcohol use for both adults and teens.

17. Married people, especially married men, have longer life expectancies than do otherwise similar singles.

18. Marriage is associated with better health and lower rates of injury, illness, and disability for both men and women.

19. Marriage seems to be associated with better health among minorities and the poor.

Mental Health and Emotional Well-being

20. Children whose parents divorce have higher rates of psychological problems like depression and other mental illnesses.

21. Divorce is linked to higher suicide rates.

22. Married mothers have lower rates of depression than do single or cohabiting mothers.

Crime and Domestic Violence

23. Boys raised in single-parent families are more likely to engage in delinquent and criminal behaviour.

24. Married men and women are significantly less likely to be the perpetrators or victims of crime.

25. Married women appear to have a lower risk of experiencing domestic violence than do cohabiting or dating women.

26. A child who is not living with his or her own two married parents is at significantly greater risk for child abuse.

Suggested Readings

This list is by no means exhaustive, but it includes some of the books and articles I have found to be the most useful, informative, and insightful. In addition to my own knowledge, these readings have provided guidance and ideas for assisting individuals/couples in my clinical practice and when offering lectures about when, whom, and why to marry or not.

Arp, D. (2003). *Ten great dates before you say I do*. Grand Rapids, MI: Zondervan.

Coontz, S. (2012). *A strange stirring: The feminine mystique and American women at the dawn of the 1960s*. New York, NY: Basic Books.

Fisher, H.E. (2010). *Why him? Why her?: Finding real love by understanding your personality type*. New York, NY: Holt Paperbacks.

George, R.P. & Elshtain, J.B. (2010). *The meaning of marriage: Family, state, market, and morals*. New York, NY: Scepter Publishers.

Gladwell, M. (2008). *Outliers: The story of*

success. New York, NY: Penguin Books.

Glass, S. (2003). *Not "just friends": Rebuilding trust and recovering your sanity after infidelity.* New York, NY: Simon & Schuster, Inc.

Gottman, J. & Silver, N. (2000). *The seven principles for making marriage work: A practical guide from the country's foremost relationship expert.* New York, NY: Three Rivers Press.

Gottman, J., Schwartz Gottman, J., & Declaire, J. (2007). *Ten lessons to transform your marriage: America's love lab experts share their strategies for strengthening your relationship.* New York, NY: Three Rivers Press.

Gottman, J. & DeClaire, J. (2001). *The relationship cure: A 5 step guide to strengthening your marriage, family, and friendships.* New York, NY: Three Rivers Press.

Gottman, J. (2012). *What makes love last? How to build trust and avoid betrayal.* New York, NY: Simon and Schuster.

Gottman, J. (1994). *Why marriages succeed or fail: And how you can make yours last.* New York, NY: Fireside.

Gray, J. (1992). *Men are from Mars, Women are from Venus*. New York, NY: HarperCollins Publishers.

Hendrix, H. (2008). *Getting the love you want: A guide for couples*. New York, NY: Henry Holt and Co.

Institute for American Values.(2005). *Why Marriage Matters: Thirty Conclusions from the Social Sciences* (2nd ed.). Retrieved from http://americanvalues.org/pdfs/why_marriage_matters2.pdf.

Janmohamed, S.Z. (2009). *Love in a Headscarf*. London, England: Aurum Press Ltd.

Johnson, S. (2008). *Hold me tight: Seven conversations for a lifetime of love*. New York, NY: Little, Brown, & Co.

Love, P. & Stosny, S. (2008). *How to improve your marriage without talking about it*. New York, NY: Broadway Books.

Markman, H., Stanley, S.M., Blumberg, S.L. (2010). *Fighting for your marriage*. San Francisco, CA: Jossey-Bass.

Notarius, C. & Markman, H. (1993). *We can work it out: How to resolve conflicts, save your marriage*. New York, NY: The Berkley Publishing Co.

Oppenheimer, V. K. (2003). Cohabiting and marriage during young men's career development process. *Demography, 40 (1),* 127-149.

Perel, E. (2007). *Mating in captivity: Unlocking erotic intelligence.* New York, NY: HarperCollins.

Parker-Pope, T. (2010). *For better: The science of a good marriage.* Boston, MA: Dutton.

Raskin, V.D. (2003). *Great sex for moms: Ten steps to nurturing passion while raising kids.* New York, NY: Touchstone.

Real, T. (2002). *How can I get through to you? Closing the intimacy gap between men and women.* New York, NY: Scribner.

Real, T. (2008). *The new rules of marriage: What you need to know to make love work.* New York, NY: Ballantine Books.

Spring, J.A. (2005). *How can I forgive you?: The courage to forgive, the freedom not to.* New York, NY: Avon.

Stanley, S., Rhoades, G.K., & Markham, H.J. (2006). Sliding versus deciding: Inertia and the premarital cohabitation effect. *Family Relations, 55,* 499-509.

Stosny, S. (2006). *Love without hurt: Turn your resentful, angry, or emotionally abusive relationship into a compassionate, loving one*. New York, NY: Simon & Schuster, Inc.

Waite, L. & Gallagher, M. (2001). *The case for marriage: Why married people are happier, healthier, and better off financially*. New York, NY: Random House.

Watson, W.L. (2001). *Purity and passion: Spiritual truths about intimacy that will strengthen your marriage*. Salt Lake City, UT: Deseret Book Company.

Weiner-Davis, M. (1992). *Divorce busting: A step-by-step approach to making your marriage loving again*. New York, NY: Simon & Shuster.

Weiner-Davis, M. (2003). *The sex-starved marriage: A couple's guide to boosting their marriage libido*. New York, NY: Simon & Schuster.

Whitehead, B.D. (2003). *Why there are no good men Left: The romantic plight of the new single woman*. New York, NY: Broadway Books. (2005). *Conclusions*

Willoughby, B.J., Olson, C.D., Carroll, J.S., Nelson, L.J., & Miller, R.B. (2012). Sooner or later? The marital horizons of parents and their emerging adult children. *Journal of Social and Personal Relationships, 29 (7)*, 967-981.

Wright, L.M. (2005). Marriage: It matters in sickness and in health. *Journal of Family Nursing, 11(4)*, 1-7.

Wright, L.M. (2005). *Spirituality, suffering, and illness: Ideas for healing.* Philadelphia, PA: FA Davis.

Wright, L.M. & Bell, J.M. (2009). *Beliefs and illness: A model for healing.* Calgary, AB: 4th Floor Press.

Wright, L.M. & Leahey, M. (2013). *Nurses and families: A guide to family assessment and intervention* (6th ed.). Philadelphia, PA: FA Davis.

Movies That Celebrate Marriage

Often a line from a movie can resonate within you and stay with you forever. One of the most beautiful dialogue passages in a movie that celebrates marriage comes from the poignant Japanese movie *Shall We Dance* (Fields, Wells, & Chelsom, 2004). In the English version, the wife, played by Susan Sarandon, asks: "Why do we marry? We marry because we need a witness to our lives. There are a billion people on the planet, what does any one life really mean? But in a marriage you are promising to care about everything, the good things, the bad things, the terrible things, the mundane things, all of them, all the time, everyday! You are saying your life will not go unnoticed, because I will notice it, your life will not go unwitnessed because I will be your witness."

Below is a list of sixteen movies that celebrate marriage. I recommend them as a great idea for a date night!

AMOUR
Haneke, M.; Menegoz, M.; Arndt, S.; Heiduschka, V.; Katz, M. (Producers) & Haneke, M. (Director). (2012). *Amour* [motion picture]. France: Sony Pictures Classics.

ANOTHER YEAR
Brandon, D., Egan, G., Lowe, G., Ross, T. (Producers) & Leigh, M. (Director). (2010). *Another Year*. UK: Sony Pictures Classics.

AWAY FROM HER
Egoyan, A., Hirst, V., Iron, D., Mankoff, D., Urdl, S., Weiss, J. (Producers) & Polley, S. (Director). (2006). *Away from Her*. Canada, UK & USA: The Film Farm & Foundry Films.

DEPARTURES
Mase, Y., Nakazawa, T., Nobukuni, I., Watai, T. (Producers) & Takita, Y. (Director). (2008). *Departures*. Japan: Amuse Soft Entertainment.

FATHER OF THE BRIDE
Baum, C., Block, B., Cruickshank, J., Gallin, S., Meyers, N., Orr, J., Rosenman, H., Williams, C. (Producers) & Shyer, C. (Director). (1991). *Father of the Bride* [motion picture]. USA: Sandollar Productions, Touchstone Pictures & Touchwood Pacific Partners.

GUESS WHO'S COMING TO DINNER

Glass, G. (Producer) & Kramer, S. (Producer\/ Director). (1967). *Guess Who's Coming to Dinner?* [motion picture]. USA: Columbia Pictures Corporation.

HOPE SPRINGS

Bell, B., Black, T., Blumenthal, J., Casady, G., Coggins, C., Grey, L., Harlacker, J., Johnson, L., Kahane, N., Konop, K., Nelson, J., Norris, R., Tisch, S. (Producers) & Frankel, D. (Director). (2012). *Hope Springs*. USA: Columbia Pictures.

IRIS

Dreyer, M., East, G., Fox, R., Hedley, T., Minghella, A., Pollack, S., Rudin, S., Thompson, D., Weinstein, H. (Producers) & Eyre, R. (Director). (2001). *Iris*. Uk & USA: British Broadcasting Corporation (BBC), Fox Iris Productions, Intermedia Films, Mirage Enterprises & Miramax Films.

JULIE & JULIA

Bernard, J., Dreyer, D., Ephron, N., Lee Jr, D., Mark, L., Robinson, A., Rudin, S., Sacha, J.J., Steel, E., Stevens, D. (Producers) & Ephron, N. (Director). (2009). *Julie and Julia* [motion picture]. USA: Columbia Pictures.

SHADOWLANDS

Attenborough, R., Clegg, T., Eastman, B., Hawkins, D., Webb, A. (Producers) & Attenborough, R. (Director). (1993). *Shadowlands* [motion picture]. UK: Price Entertainment.

SHALL WE DANCE?
Berman, J., Fields, S., Goldstein, J., Hudgins, R., Israel, A., Osher, B., Snyder Johnson, M., Weinstein, B., Weinstein, H., Winkler, M. (Producers) & Chelsom, P. (Director). (2004). *Shall We Dance?* [motion picture]. USA: Miramax.

THE NOTEBOOK
Emmerich, T., Harris, L., Johnson, M., Kaplan, A. (Producers) & Cassavetes, N. (Director). (2004). *The Notebook* [motion picture]. USA: New Line Cinema.

THE THING ABOUT MY FOLKS
Gaub, S., Newmyer, R., Reiser, P., Silver, J., Zelermyer, J. (Producers) & De Felitta, R. (Director). (2005). *The Thing about My Folks*. USA: New Line Cinema.

UP
Lasseter, J., Rae, K., Ream, D., Rivera, J., Stanton, A. (Producers) & Docter, P., Peterson, B. (Directors). (2009). *Up* [motion picture]. USA: Walt Disney Pictures & Pixar Animation Studio.

WALK THE LINE

Blomquist, A., Carter Cash, J., Keach, J., Konrad, K. Robin, L. (Producers) & Mangold, J. (Director). (2005). *Walk the Line* [motion picture]. USA & Germany: 20th Century Fox [br] & Twentieth Century Fox [us].

WHEN HARRY MET SALLY

Ephron, N., Nicolaides, S., Reiner, R., Scheinman, A., Stott, J. (Producers) & Reiner, R. (Director). (1989). *When Harry Met Sally* [motion picture]. USA: MGM.

ABOUT THE AUTHOR

Lorraine M. Wright, RN, PhD, completed her doctoral studies in marriage and family therapy and has been a practicing marriage and family consultant/therapist for forty years. Her expertise in marriage and family relationships also extends to couples and families suffering with serious illness by combining her original discipline of nursing with marriage and family therapy. Dr. Wright is also an author, blogger, and international speaker. She is a Professor Emeritus of Nursing, University of Calgary, Canada, where for twenty years she directed an outpatient clinic, the Family Nursing Unit, for couples/families suffering with serious illness. In addition, she has co-written nine professional books and numerous book chapters and articles. Dr. Wright has received several honours and awards for her distinguished contributions and leadership in family nursing and marital and family therapy from the American Association for Marriage and Family Therapy, the American Family Therapy Academy, and the International Family Nursing

Conference. Dr. Wright has received two honourary doctorates from the University of Montreal, Canada, 2008, and Linnaeus University, Kalmar, Sweden, 2012. Most recently in 2013, she was awarded a Queen Elizabeth II Diamond Jubilee Medal in Canada. She is a much sought after speaker and has offered keynotes, lectures, workshops, and consultations in thirty countries.

AUTHOR CONTACT INFORMATION

Lorraine M. Wright, RN, PhD

Book website: www.notmarryunless.com

Contact me for information about face-to-face, telephone, or online individual/couples therapy if you are

- struggling and/or suffering whether to enter a marriage;
- struggling and/or suffering about whether to exit a marriage;
- struggling and/or suffering with how to fortify your marriage.

Contact me for lectures, workshops, keynote addresses, and/or consultations related to the following topics:

- Don't Get Married . . . Unless;
- Three Pillars for Fortifying Your Marriage;

- Illness Suffering and Family Healing;

- Spirituality, Suffering, and Illness;

- Clinical Practice Models for Health Professionals

(Illness Beliefs Model; Trinity Model: Calgary Family Assessment and Intervention Models).

Email: lmwright@ucalgary.ca

Blog: www.lorrainewright.com/blog

Twitter: @drlorwright

Websites:

www.lorrainewright.com;

www.IllnessBeliefsModel.com

www.FamilyNursingResources.com;

www.SpiritualitySufferingandIllness.com